*My One Word* is a refreshing approach to New Year's resolutions, replacing unrealistic goals with the desire to become a more committed disciple of the Lord Jesus Christ. I commend Mike Ashcraft and Rachel Olsen for focusing the reader's mind on the only true Word that can change a resolution into a reality.

— Franklin Graham,
president & CEO of Samaritan's Purse and
the Billy Graham Evangelistic Association

You are only one decision away from a totally different life. One change in spiritual disciplines can open up new dimensions of grace and power. Use *My One Word* to stop repeating the past and start creating the future.

— Mark Batterson, author of *New York Times*
bestseller *The Circle Maker* and lead pastor
of National Community Church

*My One Word* is a lens that can change every area of your life. This is more than a to-do list and more than a New Year's resolution. This can be a lifestyle with pretty dramatic results.

—Kyle Idleman, author of *Not A Fan*
and teaching pastor of Southeast Christian Church

I love the simplicity of choosing one word for the year and letting God marinate me in every aspect of that word for 365 days. *My One Word* gives folks a practical road map to do just that. Read it, apply it, and see your life and world change.

— Mary DeMuth, author of *Everything: What You Give
and What You Gain to Become Like Jesus*

Martin Luther famously said that God overturned all of Satan's work in his heart through the louder word of the gospel. My friend Mike Ashcraft has shown us how single gospel-based words can renew our hearts and refocus our lives.

— J.D. Greear, lead pastor of the Summit Church,
author of *Gospel: Recovering the Power That Made Christianity Revolutionary*

*My One Word* is more than a book; it is a life-defining experience. I've used the "one word" concept in my personal life, business life, and prayer life — and found it to be doable and inspirational. Much more than a mere New Year's resolution, choosing one word shapes the way you think and heightens your focus, helping you become all that you are called to be.

— Marybeth Whalen, author of *The Guest Book*
and director of SheReads.org

Finding focus in this fast-paced world can be a struggle, but here's a simple solution: one word. In *My One Word*, Ashcraft and Olsen lead readers through a process of selecting one word that will provide focus for the year. Creating that clear vision can eliminate distractions and free a person to quiet the clamor, listen attentively to God, and respond in faith. Give it a try. You may find that a singular focus for the year keeps you in constant contact with the sweetest word of all: *Jesus.*

— Ann Kroeker, author of *Not So Fast: Slow-Down Solutions for Frenzied Families*

CHANGE YOUR LIFE WITH JUST ONE WORD

# MY ONE WORD

MIKE ASHCRAFT & RACHEL OLSEN

ZONDERVAN®

ZONDERVAN

*My One Word*



Requests for information should be addressed to:
Zondervan, 3900 *Sparks Dr. SE, Grand Rapids, Michigan 49546*

Library of Congress Cataloging-in-Publication Data

Ashcraft, Mike, 1970-
My one word : change your life with just one word / Mike Ashcraft and Rachel Olsen.
p. cm.
ISBN 978-0-310-31877-4 (softcover)
1. Change (Psychology)—Religious aspects—Christianity. 2. Spiritual formation. 3. Attention—Religious aspects—Christianity. 4. Focus (Linguistics)
I. Olsen, Rachel, 1970- II. Title.
BV4599.5.C44A84 2013
248.4—dc23 2012030902



Published in association with William K. Jensen Literary Agency.

*Cover design: Curt Diepenhorst*
*Cover photography: Shutterstock®*
*Interior illustration: iStockphoto®*
*Interior design: Katherine Lloyd, The DESK*

*Printed in the United States of America*

First printing October 2012 / Printed in the United States of America

To the body of believers
at Port City Community Church

■ ■ ■

And to the thousands everywhere
who've joined us on the My One Word journey

# CONTENTS


Acknowledgments . . . . . . . . . . . . . . . . . . . . . . . . . . 9

Introduction: Words Have Power . . . . . . . . . . . . . . . . . 13

1. What Is My One Word? . . . . . . . . . . . . . . . . . . . . . 17
2. Beyond Self-Help . . . . . . . . . . . . . . . . . . . . . . . . 27
3. Pick Your Word . . . . . . . . . . . . . . . . . . . . . . . . . 43
4. Self-Deception . . . . . . . . . . . . . . . . . . . . . . . . . 53
5. Keep It in Front of You . . . . . . . . . . . . . . . . . . . . 67
6. Hearing Isn't the Hard Part . . . . . . . . . . . . . . . . . . 77
7. Let It Morph . . . . . . . . . . . . . . . . . . . . . . . . . . 93
8. Seeing Through Your Word . . . . . . . . . . . . . . . . . . . 103
9. Blow Up the Moment . . . . . . . . . . . . . . . . . . . . . . 117
10. Write Your Guts Out . . . . . . . . . . . . . . . . . . . . . 131
11. Wait for It . . . . . . . . . . . . . . . . . . . . . . . . . . 149
12. Last Words . . . . . . . . . . . . . . . . . . . . . . . . . . 165

Video Discussion Guide . . . . . . . . . . . . . . . . . . . . . . 181

# ACKNOWLEDGMENTS

I've read acknowledgments in other books, and the common sentiment seems to be that words aren't enough to say thanks. At the completion of this book, I know what they mean. Words are not enough, but I do want to try to say thanks to a few people.

First, I am grateful to the congregation of Port City Community Church. We continue to discover what it looks like to live by faith and help each other walk with God each step of the way!

Thanks to Sarah Beakes for calling K-LOVE. Also to Evan Vetter, Mike Paschal, Warren King, Tony Ripa, and Rachael Dowdy for their encouragement, feedback, and vision for this project.

To the Leadership Team, the Board of Directors, and the staff of Port City Community Church for their constant encouragement and support for this project.

To Rick and Rachel Olsen, thank you for helping me to make sense and complete sentences. Rick, thanks for sharing your family, and Rachel, thanks for sharing your gifts (not only your writing, but teaching me to write!).

To my family—the Ashcrafts, the Austins, the Kuhnes, and the Lloyds—thanks for your prayers, your support, and for keeping me straight.

To my two beautiful girls, who sacrificed a lot of "daddy-time" but always let me know how proud you were as I wrote—I am proud of both of you!

And everyone knows that the toughest job at a church is not

being a pastor but, rather, being a pastor's wife. Julie, thank you for being the best friend I could ever ask for. I couldn't imagine doing this without your support. I loved sharing a word with you and love sharing my life with you. *Thank you* doesn't begin to cover it.

Thank you to everyone who takes the time to read this book and who takes it seriously enough to pick a word. May God honor your efforts and change your life!

— Mike Ashcraft

■ ■ ■

It's easy to identify who I most need to thank for the opportunity to create this book. But as Mike said, it's hard to thank them adequately. My thanks go …

First and foremost, to God — who created me anew in Christ Jesus to do the good things he planned for me long ago.

Second, to my husband, Rick, who regularly bends over backward to support those plans God has. I couldn't ask for a better match or a bigger supporter of my dreams. I treasure you.

To my children, Alaina and Caleb, who not only accommodated my busy schedule for a long season, but prayed for this project every single night during its creation. I love you always.

To my sweet P31 teamates—I appreciate you. And last, but far from least, to my pastor and coauthor Mike Ashcraft, who refused to quit no matter how many times I "made that face again" while reading through one of our rough drafts. I couldn't be more grateful for your leadership and our partnership in ministry.

— Rachel Olsen

■ ■ ■

# ACKNOWLEDGMENTS

We'd both like to thank Bill Jensen of William K. Jensen Literary Agency for his representation and ardent support. We'd also like to thank the stellar team at Zondervan, including Sandy Vander Zicht, Don Gates, Tom Dean, Robin Phillips, and T. J. Rathburn.

Finally, we'd like to thank the music of the eighties for keeping Rachel's energy up and for keeping Mike's attention-challenged self company during nearly a year's worth of coffee-shop writing sessions. We hope our readers enjoy the results.

— Mike and Rachel

# WORDS HAVE POWER

The first day of class every semester, I begin my public speaking course at the university the same way. I ask my students to take out a scrap piece of paper and tear it into three smaller pieces.

From this one exercise, I can tell what kind of person each student is. The conscientious, detail-oriented, type-A students fold their paper neatly into three equal sections. They crease each fold, then fold it back the other direction and crease again. Sliding the crease to the edge of their desk, they apply pressure for a clean, straight tear. They wind up with three perfect pieces of scrap paper — but it takes a while.

The other group — the big-picture, usually more gregarious, impulsive type-B people — quickly rip their page into three smaller sections. The edges are tattered. The pieces are uneven. They don't care about that; they don't even notice. They just want to know what we're going to do with the paper.

I instruct the class to take one piece of their scrap paper and draw a creepy bug on it — any sort of insect or arachnid you wouldn't want crawling up your leg. The type-As also take longer to draw their bugs.

Then I tell them to take the second piece of paper and write down the name of a food they hate. Any food they think has an awful taste, texture, or smell. Anything they would cringe to have to chew and swallow.

Finally, on the last piece of paper, I instruct them to write down whatever term they call their mother or the mother figure in their life. Might be a stepmother's first name or a grandmother's nickname. Most simply scribble the letters *M-o-m*.

Next I have them stand next to their desks with their three pieces of paper. I hold up my first piece, showing them my poorly illustrated picture of a centipede. I lay the paper bug on the ground and stomp it, like I'm killing it. I instruct them to follow suit with theirs.

After the briefest hesitation, the class — freshmen to seniors — begin smiling and stomping on their first piece of paper. Smashing ink-drawn spiders and roaches and fire ants over and over with their sneaker- or flip-flop-clad feet.

They laugh at themselves and each other, and I have to speak louder now to be heard over the commotion. I hold up my next piece of scrap paper, showing them the word *beets* I've written on mine. "Now throw down your second piece of paper with your food on it and stomp on it too. Because who wants to eat that?

"Yuck!" I insist as I stomp on the paper that says *beets*. They follow suit, happily stomping out broccoli and Brussels sprouts and Aunt Hilda's congealed salad. Laughing and talking and stomping, they surmise this is going to be a fun class.

With momentum running high, I hold up my third scrap of paper where I've written the word *Mom*. I shout, "Okay, now ..." to get their attention. I toss this paper down next to the other two pieces at my feet and tell them to stomp on their last piece of paper as well.

Suddenly my foot striking the floor is the only sound in the room. Motionless they stare at me stomping. Some look around the room — checking to see if others are as taken aback as they are. But none stomp, despite my repeated urgings.

In a decade of teaching, I've never had a class do anything

other than freeze with quizzical looks when I tell them to step on the third piece of paper.

Why? Well, that's what I explain next so the students will grasp the tremendous power, value, and responsibility of public speaking. Of any kind of speaking, really.

Of words, essentially.

I tell them that they don't tread on that little piece of paper with the word *Mom* because words are more than collections of letters. They are not just lines and curves. They represent.

It doesn't matter that their mothers aren't in the room to witness their stomping. I usually tell them that if their mother were present, she'd tell them to obey their teacher. They smile at that irony, but they still don't stomp.

It doesn't matter that each of them at some point in their life have felt like stomping when it comes to their mother. They've all been toddlers and teens. This doesn't matter, because the word *Mom* not only represents their mother, but the role of mother. The idea of mom. The office and calling of motherhood.

In essence I've asked them to stomp on all that is loving, nurturing, live-giving, and good. As if it were an ant or an anchovy. I tell them stomping on that word felt wrong because words encapsulate ideas. They evoke our emotions. They hook into memories. They define our experiences — helping to shape us in the process.

There's power in words. Beauty in words. Grace in words.

Words create movement. They craft nations. They seal a marriage. They cast vision. They make us laugh. They focus our attention. They expand our horizons. They stimulate our creativity. And they script our possibilities.

That's why I'm so excited you've picked up this book. Inside these pages we will walk you through the process of using one word in the coming year to effect personal change and spiritual formation.

This is a simple but potent practice. Don't assume its simplicity limits its effectiveness. If you enter fully into the My One Word process, one simple word will reach farther into your life and embed deeper into your character than you've ever imagined it could.

I've done this My One Word project for six years now with my pastor, Mike Ashcraft, and the body of believers at Port City Community Church. So when Mike asked me to coauthor this book about the My One Word project, I didn't hesitate, because I know firsthand what this exercise can do. That's why I'm excited for you, and what the coming year holds as you participate in this with us.

I can't wait for you to see how one word can profoundly change your life!

— Rachel Olsen

## Chapter 1

# WHAT IS MY ONE WORD?

*So teach us to number our days,*
*that we may present to You a heart of wisdom.*
— Psalm 90:12 NASB

I don't have enough time to live my own life!

I reached this conclusion after trying to follow all the advice given on a morning news show one week in January.

It seemed like a smart way to start my day. I figured I'd tune in, get the forecast, learn the headlines, and maybe hear a celebrity interview. I wasn't expecting all the show segments telling me how to live my life better.

Most of these segments offered the promise of deliverance: "Financial Freedom Is Closer than You Think" or "Four Secrets to Better Communication." Others, I decided, were designed to scare the socks off of me: "Six Health Risks Every Person Faces" or "Thieves You Cannot See — Avoiding Identity Theft."

Motivated by this combination of hope and fear, I compiled a to-do list of ways to improve my life and its management according to the experts. The more I listened, learned, and listed, the more behind schedule I felt.

The topics on my list ranged from health maintenance to home maintenance to car maintenance. I was informed I need to eat certain foods every day: four veggies, three fruits, two proteins (preferably chicken or fish), and I think a partridge in a pear tree. I also need to get enough fiber, calcium, Vitamin D, B, C, and Beta-something-or-other.

I need thirty minutes of cardio a day (but apparently with the right exercise product this can be done in ten), fifteen minutes of strength training, and ten minutes of stretching. Plus, some extended time for meditation so that my body and mind could align. I'm told a germ-resistant mat is needed for that.

I need to bust my stress, nurture my creativity, and improve my posture.

I need to pay attention to my finances. Save and invest. Spend frugally — yet somehow also buy the cool gadgets they review on the show. Apparently extreme couponing is the way to afford it all, but it takes a lot of time to save 80 percent on your grocery bill.

I need to check my credit report regularly. Shred important documents. Back up my computer. Meet with my financial planner. And read the information that comes with our kid's (underfunded) college fund. That, by the way, is forty pages of legal and financial mumbo jumbo in eight-point font, single-spaced. I suppose I need to meet with my attorney to understand it.

And that creates two prerequisite tasks to add to the list: find an attorney and find a financial planner. They assume every regular Joe has a CFP, a CPA, and a JD on speed dial. I have Domino's on mine.

The list continues.

Change my oil every 3,000 miles and my transmission fluid every 30,000. Test my smoke detector batteries biannually. Change my air filters every other month. Replace my toothbrush every three months. Flip my mattress every six. Buy new pillows every three years—I think this is for my posture, but it could be to get rid of dust mites.

Check my skin for irregular moles. Check my yard for moles too. Weed and feed the lawn each spring. Grow houseplants to cleanse the air.

Save last night's roasted chicken bones to make my own chicken stock. Buy undervalued international stocks. Sell my stock before it drops. And stock my pantry for possible natural disasters.

Fertilize, amortize, winterize, maximize, scrutinize. Suddenly I realized: I don't have time to live my life!

### PAUSE

My word for the year is PAUSE. In my busy life there are so many times I need to pause. Pause to remember these days, for they will fly by so quickly. Pause to say yes ... and no. Pause to give thanks. Pause before I speak in anger, judgment, or criticism. Pause to say I'm sorry. Pause to dwell on God's goodness and mercy.

*—Dawn*

Looking at the list of things I was supposed to do to live my life right, or well, or whatever all this was going to do for me, I felt defeated. The list that was going to improve my life left me overwhelmed.

In my moment of defeat all I wanted to do was go surf. 'Course the list said I should put on a high-SPF sunscreen and take along a BPA-free water bottle to keep me well hydrated. Filled with filtered spring water, of course.

### *Dropping the Ball*

I'm sure you can relate; you've made lists too. Lists of things you want to start doing or stop doing—things you want to change about yourself. Lists of ways to improve your life and your character.

Maybe you've only listed them in your head. But I bet they come to mind each January. Nearly two-thirds of America's population has made New Year's resolutions.[1] I am one of them.

And you've probably found, like I've found, that each day keeps blurring into the next while we try to make some progress with our many good intentions. Yet very little actually changes.

That ball keeps dropping in Times Square each New Year's. And we keep dropping the ball on our resolutions to improve. Only 20 percent of resolution makers report achieving any significant long-term change.[2]

When I open my Bible, I find more lists. Things a follower of Christ should do. Things a follower of Christ should resist doing. Traits a follower of Christ should display — all the truly important stuff that never makes it onto morning show segments.

When was I going to get to *any* of this?

I decided to drop my list of ways to get the most out of my life. I realized I needed to find a new way to approach personal change.

### *Losing the List, Picking a Word*

My first journal entry in 2004 was a single word: FLOW. Not merely written on the page, but etched in bubble letters about three-quarters of an inch tall. The letters are heavily outlined, surrounded by a thin border, and colored in gray.

It took me about ten minutes to draw and color the word FLOW. But it took three weeks to narrow all that was bubbling up in me down to that single word.

---

1 Barna Research Group, January 3, 2011, http://www.barna.org/culture-articles/465-americans-resolutions-for-2011

2 Ibid.

I'd been writing in a journal for years, but here was something I had never done before. Instead of blasting paragraphs on a page to capture my thoughts and insights, recording my steps and setbacks, I decided to meditate on just one word.

I wrote this word FLOW in response to something Jesus said. He said, "Whoever believes in me, as the Scripture has said, 'Out of his heart will flow rivers of living water' " (John 7:38 ESV). That struck a nerve.

There were times when I felt the living water flowing with ease from my heart. But there were other times, more times, when it felt forced.

The idea of FLOW drew me forward. It didn't have the trappings of regret or the pressure of sweeping promises to change like my resolutions did. It awakened something in me. Not a compulsive desire to change born out of being sick of the way I was, but a desire to live an authentic life that flowed from my relationship with Christ.

Could my life really flow from my heart? The question sent me on a search anchored by the four letters of this one word. If what Jesus said was true — pause for the obvious answer to arise — then I'd need a way to pay attention to my heart on a daily basis.

I decided looking at and concentrating on this word FLOW would remind me to do that. In the months to come, I paid attention to FLOW and used it to gauge my heart and my life. I discovered I could tell the condition of my heart based on what was coming out of it into my life.

And slowly, over time with this word FLOW, I learned to reverse that process. Instead of looking at my life and actions to realize the state of my heart, I proactively addressed the condition of my heart. That changed my life.

In looking through the lens of a single chosen word, I found a new approach to personal change and spiritual formation — one that is doable, memorable, effective, and sticky. The results have been greater than I expected.

### FAITHFUL

For twenty-seven years I've believed that my plan for my life is superior to God's plan. My time has been spent pursuing goals, accomplishments, and things I felt I needed to be happy and complete. After twenty-seven years of much external success, I realized I was still personally and emotionally unsatisfied. While driving to work one morning I was listening to K-LOVE, and I heard Mike talk of the One Word concept. That day I decided, for the first time in my life, to focus on God's plan for my life instead of my own. Handing over the reins has not been easy; in fact, sometimes I'm not sure I have the endurance. So I chose FAITHFUL as my one word, because I'm committed to being faithful to God's Word and plan. The thought of where things are going is exciting! I'm now being led by the earth's Creator.

*—Brian*

## *A Movement Rises*

In January of 2007, I challenged my church, Port City Community Church in Wilmington, North Carolina, to ditch their New Year's resolutions and each pick a word to focus on that year. I titled the series and the project "My One Word." People quickly embraced it. Within a few years, My One Word embedded itself into the DNA of our church. It's how we now approach personal change and spiritual growth.

One of the coolest things to me is how My One Word not only gives people a doable way to focus on their spiritual formation, but an easy way to talk about it. Around here you'll hear people asking each other, "What's your word?" or, "How's it going with your one word?" You'll hear them answer, "My one word is ___, and so far God's been showing me ____."

Couples, family, and friends all help hold each other accountable, simply by talking about their words — around the dinner table, at small group meetings, even on Facebook.

In January 2009, the nation's most notable Christian radio station called my office. K-LOVE had heard about My One Word and invited me to come on the air to tell their listeners about the project. I shared My One Word with half a million listeners that month. And I returned to the K-LOVE airways to talk about My One Word in 2010 and throughout 2011. A movement caught fire.

The movement didn't become a movement because K-LOVE called me, but because God has called each of us. This is not a movement of me or my church, but a movement of God. And of his people wanting to be transformed into his image.

## *Focus Is Required*

Our lives are fast-paced and demanding. Our attention is divided. The normal, natural pace of our lives will not likely lead us toward spiritual formation. We have so many things to focus on that spiritual formation tends to fall to the wayside, along with our good intentions to rotate our mattress or wax our cars.

Most of us feel overwhelmed at the idea of embarking on a grand plan for spiritual formation like reading through the Bible in a year or memorizing a verse every week. We'd like to, but it just hasn't happened. Enter My One Word. It's easy, doable, and surprisingly powerful, mainly because it supplies narrowed focus.

This book will give you a simple but effective plan to effect personal change (spiritual formation) by allowing a single word to become the lens through which you examine your heart and life for an entire year.

Your single word will force clarity and concentrate your efforts. And as you focus on your word over an extended period of time, you position yourself for God to form your character at a deep, sustainable level.

### BOLDNESS

I saw the myoneword.org site on a friend's Facebook page and checked it out. Immediately after reading the purpose behind My One Word, a word popped into my head. I sat at my desk trying to think of a different trait to focus on. I read through other people's words to see if I could scavenge a good one off their list. I didn't want to use the word God gave me, because it was terrifying to me. Which was silly, because it's just a word. But at the same time, knowing that I'd be accountable to it for a year—that's rough stuff.

I am an intensely shy person. I avoid confrontation at all costs. And I only share my faith when it happens into a conversation. The idea of BOLDNESS, of being a truly bold Christian, is seriously out of my comfort zone. But it seems that this is God's challenge for me this year. I am to actively pursue BOLDNESS and be transformed in the process. So here I go—man, this is intimidating!

*—Jen*

We're so busy with the surface-level things of life that we forget to number our days and tend to our hearts. We become so preoccupied with getting our lives to a manageable point or a better future that we miss both the moment right now and the reality of a coming eternity.

Yet God calls us to use our days to develop a heart of wisdom. And that's what this My One Word project is ultimately about.

Between these pages I'll outline how to pick a word for the

year and how to focus on it. I'll discuss what you can do to drive it deep into your character and what you can do to apply it in your life. The goal is a transformed heart.

At the close of each chapter you'll find directions and questions for personal reflection. Grab a journal and spend some time with the questions to help you get the most out of your year with your one word.

Throughout each chapter you'll also see words chosen by men and women from all walks of life — college students, pastors, moms, recovering drug addicts. You'll hear their reasons for choosing their one word and their experience with this project. I think you'll find those inspiring.

I invite you to join us this year on the My One Word journey. Change is possible. But focus is required. It's time to get single-minded and single-worded about your resolution to change. Are you ready? Well then, keep reading!

## *Reflect*

- What are some things you would like to change about yourself?
- What distracts you from focusing on the change or the spiritual formation you desire?
- Think about your past attempts to change. Have you made resolutions or sweeping promises to change? How well did it work?
- Often our desire to change is fueled by regret — does regret generally propel you forward or hold you back?

## Chapter 2

# BEYOND SELF-HELP

*Are you so foolish? Having begun by the Spirit, are you now being perfected by the flesh?*

— Galatians 3:3 ESV

I guess I should be thankful my neighbor didn't have a gun.

It was just after 5:30 p.m. on Friday, Memorial Day weekend. My daughter was turning six the following day, and we were hosting her birthday party at the house we'd just moved into.

The house had sat vacant, and the yard was covered in leaves, sticks, and pine needles from numerous surrounding trees. So my friend Derek, who owns his own landscape business, came over after work with his high-powered tools to help me whip the yard into shape.

Derek strapped his professional backpack blower on me and turned it on. The nine-thousand-horsepower motor threatened to turn me into rocket man. It also threatened to deafen me.

I walked around the property blowing the clippings Derek had mulched with his industrial mower. I aimed for the beds in front of the ten-foot hedges that were growing along the privacy fence in our side yard.

Unbeknownst to me, my neighbor was some fifty feet away on the patio in her backyard, which was on the other side of the fence and hedges. And the jetpack I wore sounded loud to her too.

So as I'm blowing leaves I notice a woman walking up my driveway. I figure she's a homeowner coming to meet the new neighbors — it's probably been a while since they've heard any sounds coming from my side of the fence.

Her arms are flailing. Her mouth is moving. But I can't hear a word over the sound of the motor on my back. It wasn't quite as loud as the Third Day concert I once attended, but it was close.

I'm smiling at her, but I don't know how to turn the blower off. So she has to stand there a minute — she's yelling over the sound of the motor — until I get it shut off. Once it's off I hear what she's saying: I'm stirring up dust. I'm making lots of noise. She's trying to cook out. Why am I not more courteous and considerate? And she is really upset about this.

She ends emphatically with, "I'm so mad, if I had a gun I would shoot you!"

What does one say to that?

"I'm really sorry to have upset you, ma'am. I didn't mean to cause trouble. We'll be glad to stop."

She skulked away as I went to tell Derek to cool it. By now my wife and two girls were watching the scene from the porch, my youngest having announced, "Mama, some woman is yelling at Daddy!"

Derek made a valid point that the playground was still covered in debris. "You've got to get it clean for the kids to use it safely tomorrow." Now I had to choose between risking the injury of a small child or being shot by my new neighbor should she locate a gun when she heard me turn this thing back on.

With her threat in mind, I passed the tall hedges to an area where the fence was lower, caught her eye, and waved her over.

"Ma'am, I just want to let you know that we need to turn on the blower for a few more minutes to clean the playground off so the kids can use it at a birthday party tomorrow. But I didn't want you to think we were ignoring your request to quiet down. It won't take long at all."

With eyebrows raised, she replied in a less-than-gracious tone, "It's 5:30 on a Friday, don't you want to go home?"

"I *am* home," I said.

That's when her expression fell.

And that's when I realized she'd thought I was a hired hand.

"You're the pastor at Port City Community Church, aren't you?"

I've noticed people always seem to know when a pastor moves into the neighborhood. Word spreads fast.

"Yes, ma'am."

"You probably think I'm not even a Christian. Well, I am."

She was clearly mortified. And I couldn't decide which was more uncomfortable for me — this moment, or the one earlier when she'd wanted to kill me because I was disturbing her BBQ.

In that moment we both came face-to-face with the present condition of her heart.

"I'm not thinking you can't be a Christian," I said. Then I smiled, extended my hand over the fence, and said, "Hi, I'm Mike Ashcraft."

She grasped my hand and shook it. "Go ahead and do whatever you need to do." I could tell she just wanted me to walk away and leave her alone with her embarrassment.

Not only did she want to kill me for doing yard work on a Friday afternoon; she only regretted it when she learned I was a pastor — the new neighbor — and not the hired help.

I've often wondered what she thought or prayed after that incident. I'm pretty sure she regretted it for a long time. The only other time she spoke to me was when we bumped into each other in a local coffee shop.

## KNUCKLEHEAD

Hey, KNUCKLEHEAD. Quit worrying about tomorrow. Turn around. Look at the path you've taken. Look how God has taken care of you. Look what he has done for you to get you to where you are. It wasn't by your effort. It was his. Quit trying to rely on yourself. Look at your wonderful wife and brilliant kids. Do you really think you could've pulled that off by yourself? Sometimes when you're in a good mood and everything is going well, you praise God. But when you're worried about finances or the Red Sea, you revert to your old ways. You think, "What can I do to make it better?" Nothing. You can do nothing. Let God do it, KNUCKLEHEAD.

*—Jeff*

But here's the thing. We've all had moments when our words or actions were less than Christlike, and we were embarrassed by it. *I can't believe I just said that. I can't believe I said that in front of them. I can't believe this is happening. I hope they don't know I'm a Christian!*

In these moments we come face-to-face with the true condition of our hearts.

And what do we do when we're put into a position to see ourselves as we really are? We resolve to change. We try hard to change. When it doesn't work, we try harder. We go to the self-help section of the library. And if we get really desperate, we ask God for help.

### *The Appeal of Self-Help*

The self-help section of my local library sits right next to the spirituality section—I notice more people browse the self-help shelves. You may be thinking this book belongs on those shelves. Let me tell you why this is not a self-help book.

Self-help is a popular idea and, on the surface, a source of comfort. The concept implies that we can become whatever we want to become. Without help from anyone, except perhaps a book writer. This speaks to the essence of what we long for: to be the self-made man or woman. It is, after all, the American Dream.

Now I am all for America and all for dreams, but this desire for knowledgeable self-sufficiency isn't all it's cracked up to be. Case in point: it helped pave the way for sin to enter the world. The lure of knowing all God knows drew Eve into thinking she could then do this herself. Dependence on her Creator seemed limiting, not freeing.

Lest you think I'm throwing Eve under the bus, we all follow in her footsteps seeking knowledge that will empower us apart from God. We relegate him to certain times or spaces in our lives — like a particular library shelf to be visited — insisting on handling the rest by ourselves.

We fail to realize that building a life apart from God would mean, well, a life apart from God.

The "self-made" descriptor is revered. It's impressive. It makes us look good to others and feel good about ourselves. The problem is we are not self-made. None of us.

To claim we can make ourselves into anything we want is to deny that we are the created, not the Creator. Reality is we are made by God, for his purposes. How much potential can we truly have apart from him?

Plenty of us acknowledge this truth but still operate as if spiritual formation is something we manage to do for God — to show him our love and commitment. And we believe that when we show him our love and commitment, he lends us a helping hand.

## *Who Does God Help?*

I read an article several years ago claiming the saying, "God helps those who help themselves" is the most commonly quoted verse in the Bible. There's a problem with that claim; it's not in the Bible.

It sounds rational and seems like it belongs in there. If we demonstrate some effort to improve, God will give us a little push in that direction. If we can show him we're really serious — and at least somewhat competent — then surely he will get behind us in our attempts to change. After all, that's what he wants, right?

When we're feeling motivated to make something happen, our willpower is high. We assume he will help us because we're putting the energy forth to make a change. Besides, he's not going to waste his time putting more effort into us than we are putting into ourselves. Right?

We like grace on our terms. And we like to earn our grace, thank you very much.

We value initiative and effort in others and assume that's what God values in us too. We qualify ourselves based on how hard we work. We evaluate our character based on how often we go to church, attend Bible studies, volunteer, or check other items off on the standard religious résumé. We carry the subtle belief that God helps those who help themselves.

But when you do all these things and yet little transformation takes place, what then? Work harder? Do better? Promise to do this or swear not to do that?

We'll up our effort and willpower. DISCIPLINE is the number four most-often-picked word by My One Word devotees — and it's a great word! But it's all too easy to assume discipline is the sole solution to our problems.

## *What's the Problem?*

Dallas Willard calls spiritual transformation "the inescapable human problem with no human solution."[3] Think about that a second. He is saying you have a problem that you cannot solve. Not with more effort or education or practice or advice.

Maybe that's depressing news. Or maybe it's the best thing you've heard all day because you've struggled to change every bad habit you have to little avail.

The fact that our own spiritual transformation is a problem we can't solve indicates we need to look outside ourselves for the solution. We have to look to God.

We tend to look to God at the beginning of our walk with Christ. We hear the message of salvation — the gospel of grace that says every last one of us sins and comes up short of God's standards for righteousness. Therefore, we deserve to be left in death. But God, out of his heart of love, chose to put Christ in our place, letting him who was sinless die on the cross for our sin so we can be renewed and raised to righteousness in him.

We realize in matters of salvation that it's totally God who makes that happen, and we bow and accept it in faith. But in matters of sanctification — in other words, in matters of becoming more like Christ or in matters of changing for the better — we tend to think it's all up to us.

Paul asked the Christ followers in the region of Galatia, "Are you so foolish? Having begun by the Spirit, are you now being perfected by the flesh?" (Galatians 3:3 NASB). In other words, you couldn't live without sinning. You couldn't save yourselves

3 Dallas Willard, *Renovation of the Heart: Putting on the Character of Christ* (Colorado Springs: NavPress, 2002), 18.

from the consequences of your sin. God did that for you. Are you now trying to live without sin without his help? Are you trying to finish what he started? Do you think you can perfect yourself by yourself?

Are you trying to do something you can't do apart from God?

## ENOUGH

Every day I go through life wondering if I have done enough. Or if I have done it well enough? Whether writing a paper for my English class or participating in dance practice ... at the end of the day, I *always* wonder, was that truly enough?

The trials I have faced in life have led me to feel such doubt in everything I do. I've never felt good enough. I am taking on this One Word challenge because not only do I want to feel good enough, but I want to remember that God is enough for me. Yes, other people matter, but at the end of the day, God is sufficient for me. Regardless of how useless and futile I may feel, I will always be enough for God, and he will always be ENOUGH for me.

—*Lakyn*

Paul challenged their thinking and he challenges ours. He questions the usual mode of achieving spiritual growth, which is namely, more effort. More willpower to make ourselves do more works and obey more rules more consistently.

Paul reminds the Galatians that God has given them his Spirit and *this*—combined with their faith, not their strenuous moral striving—is what will perfect them.

God doesn't help those who help themselves. God helps those who abide with him, those who walk with him in faith. Our efforts were never the impetus for God's transforming grace. They won't be the impetus for our changed hearts either.

The Bible says that we are justified by faith. We don't need willpower or self-effort as much as we need faith that God will accomplish in us and for us what we can't do ourselves. He is the source of what we long for and need.

Willpower and self-effort can only take us so far in our desire to change. Yes, people can make changes through sheer human will, but our efforts alone will not transform us into Christ's image. Our efforts are not the source of the change we are after; they can't be. Rather, they get us in a position for God to change us.

## *Tendon Trouble*

"Come on, Mike, you can do it. It'll be fun!"

Members of my congregation were urging me to join them on the church basketball team. Basketball isn't really my thing; I surf. But they were persistent. Besides, at thirty-four I was fairly athletic; how hard could this be?

Our church had two teams in the league, duly designated the A team and the B team. Team A was playing Team B that week. I was drafted onto the B team.

Surely that designation was arbitrary; should I have been offended?

The first thirty-nine minutes actually were fun. I made a few baskets and missed a few. I could still jump — that was refreshing. Everyone likes to think they've still got it. As the game neared the end, Team B trailed Team A.

While the clock ran down, we rallied to make a late run. My teammate tried for a three-pointer (which would have cut their lead to seventeen), but the ball bounced off the rim. I followed the shot like a good hustle player should. I like fundamentals. That's when I heard the noise.

*Pop!*

What was that?

It sounded like a rubber band snapping deep inside my head.

*That's weird*, I thought.

Then the pain registered. It felt like someone had hit me with a baseball bat in the back of my right leg. Only I didn't see anyone with a bat.

The sharp pain was accompanied by a new sensation. It felt as though something was swirling up the back of my right calf toward my knee. I was slowly dropping to the floor.

Once I was on the floor, my teammates came over to my side. "Get up, old man!"

People love giving their pastors a hard time.

I really wanted to get up, but my right foot just wouldn't work. My Achilles tendon had snapped in two like a torn rubber band. Although it felt like it had recoiled toward my knee, it was actually balled up by my heel. Nerve sensations can be deceptive. As my teammates helped me back over to the bench, playing basketball slid farther down my list of things that are not my thing.

It took surgery, casts, physical therapy, and four months' time before I was back to unassisted bipedal locomotion. But this ordeal gave me the best metaphor I know of for the My One Word project.

Before the operation, my surgeon said, "Mike, a tendon is comprised of many strands and when it breaks, it frays, kind of like the end of a mop. So you have these two mop-headed ends which have to be sewn back together. But it is not the stitches that will bring the final result. The tissue actually grows back together over time. Then it's restored back to the way it was made to be."

The surgeon was telling me that he could sew the severed tendon back together, but God would have to heal it. The doctor could cut, stitch, and cast, but he couldn't cause cells to grow. He's powerless to make two torn ends of a tendon fuse; only God came up with a process by which that happens.

All we could do is set it and then hold it in position long enough for it to grow back together as God intended.

### DEPEND

My one word is DEPEND. I was reading in the fifth chapter of Matthew this morning and was reminded that Jesus says, "Blessed are the poor in spirit, for theirs is the kingdom of heaven." I long to experience the deep humility that reminds me always, every minute, that apart from God I am spiritually impoverished and hopeless. Which, in turn, will drive me to remember always, every minute, that I must DEPEND on him in all matters, in all circumstances, for everything. I never want to go anywhere or attempt anything without him.

*—Cindy*

## *Held in Place*

First, my stitched-up tendon was held in place by a cast. Then, it was held by my foot position, which was, in turn, held by an orthopedic boot. If the boot weren't made of state-of-the-art carbon and alloy, I would've insisted it was a medieval torture device.

The boot kept my right foot pointed. This position puts the least amount of pull on the tendon while it was at its weakest. Spare me ballerina jokes; I've heard them all. But great effort and care was needed at the beginning to support the weak spot.

With each subsequent doctor's visit, a ratchet device on the boot gradually adjusted the angle of my foot closer to a normal standing position as the tendon strengthened. The process was slow, tedious, and painful, but totally necessary. Today, it's as if the injury never happened.

My foot needed to be held on the outside for the sake of the work going on on the inside. This is also true of our spiritual lives. We need a boot, so to speak. Something to hold us in a given position long enough for some specific inner work to happen. My One Word can be that tool.

Throughout the ordeal with my Achilles tendon, I also learned the power of focus. A day did not go by when I wasn't aware of the transformation occurring in my heel. The boot on my foot was an ever-present reminder of what needed to happen. And I trusted it was happening even though I couldn't see it.

The boot signaled me to stay mindful of the goal, which was restoration to God's original design. It reminded me to position myself and arrange my life to accommodate this internal work.

Likewise, in the coming months, your chosen word will help you get in a specific position and remain there long enough—dependent on God—for some internal work to be done by him. Work that only he can do.

Everything else we will say in this book rests on that foundation.

My One Word is simply a doable way to support the formation process of our hearts until we've gained the strength necessary to live fully from the inside out.

---

### FAITH

My one word is FAITH. This year is the first full year I have had Christ in my life. I wasn't sure what he could or would do for me. My marriage was failing, my finances were a mess, and I had nowhere to turn. So I turned to God. I decided to have the faith to allow Christ to work in my life. I turned my problems over to him, and of course, he came through! My husband has now started his walk with God and our marriage is thriving! Although we still don't have much money, I know God will provide all we need, and I have enough faith to not worry about it. Without faith, I would be lost. With faith, my life is fulfilled. Praise God!

*—L.M.*

## *Do What You Can*

So we are positioning ourselves to focus and depend on God's work in our hearts and lives. And the most important thing we are going to do is depend on him. We are after a transformation that we can't accomplish on our own.

Am I overstating this? Can we really not form our hearts into Christ's image by ourselves?

Try this scenario. Picture Christmas. A young boy's heart is set on the mother of all Lego adventure sets. He is handed a present from his grandmother. The box is too small to be the mother of all Lego sets, but perhaps it is the car that accompanies the set. The boy's hope is still alive.

He tears through the bow, paper flies, and ... black socks.

Black socks?

There's an awkward moment of silence as his face falls into a frown. Before he says anything, Mom instructs, "Say thank you to Grandma."

Her prompt is a preventative measure, because she knows whatever is about to come out of his mouth will indicate his disappointment, heightening the social awkwardness of the moment.

When your young heart is set on the hope of Legos and you get black socks, you can will yourself to say "Thank you," but you can't generate gratitude in that moment by simply obeying your mother. There are some things we can generate and other things we can't.

We focus on the behavior — *say thank you!*

God focuses on the heart.

We focus on the social situation — *I can't believe I said that to a pastor.*

God focuses on the spiritual condition.

We can grin and say thanks through a false smile. But only God's Spirit can form a heart of gratitude in place of a heart of stone.

Love, joy, peace, patience, kindness, goodness, faithfulness, gentleness, and self-control. These are the fruit of the Spirit Paul listed for the believers in Galatia after telling them they couldn't perfect themselves with their hard work (Galatians 5:22–23).

Any of these words are great picks for this project, by the way. But notice they are fruits of the Spirit, not of our efforts. They are by-products of walking with God in faith.

So am I overstating this? Can we really not produce such things by ourselves?

According to Jesus, no, not apart from him. Christ told his followers: "I am the vine; you are the branches. Whoever abides in me and I in him, he it is that bears much fruit, for apart from me you can do nothing" (John 15:5 ESV).

*Nothing.* It's a pretty all-encompassing word, isn't it?

But here's the deal. Jesus says, "You walk with and depend on me, and you will bear much fruit." I love the reliability of Jesus's if-then statements.

The goal this year is not for you to swear you'll do better at this or for you to promise you'll never again do that. Sweeping promises inevitably breed feelings of failure. The aim is for you to use your one word to get into a focused posture and remain there while you depend on Christ.

Change is possible. Focus is required.

And should you fall off your one-word wagon at some point, you climb back on. Not with renewed willpower so much as renewed commitment to depend on him.

## *Effort, Not Earning*

I had sympathy for my neighbor that day and no desire to make her feel any worse about the situation than she already did. I can confidently say my reaction was the result of work God has done in my own heart of stone. By the way, one year my one word was REGARD—I spent twelve months learning to regard others as more important than myself.

So to be clear, change is possible but focus is required. And dependence on God is absolutely foundational.

You will read this book, feel inspired, pick a word, and get excited to tackle your own one-word project with gusto. Great! My One Word will require some effort from you, and your excitement will carry you forward. But your effort centers on remaining in a focused position for a length of time while depending on God's ability to do in you what you cannot do for yourself.

As Dallas Willard says, "Grace is not opposed to effort, it is opposed to earning."[4]

As you choose your one word in the next chapter, keep in mind that we are going to move beyond self-help into full surrender and godly dependence.

My One Word reaches further, or perhaps deeper, than self-activity or self-help ever could. True heart-level renovation takes a Master Carpenter. One who crafted your heart from the start, then redeemed it, then began a transformation in you that he will be faithful to complete (Philippians 1:6).

Remember, your commitment to change is not a means to get God to act on your behalf. He already has.

## *Reflect*

- Are you trying to change yourself?
- Are there areas of your life or character where you are resistant to God's grace? Do you feel like you've hit a plateau in your spiritual growth? Why?

---

4 Dallas Willard, "Live Life to the Full," *Christian Herald* (April 14, 2001), http://www.dwillard.org/articles/artview.asp?artID=5

- How can we know when to relax and trust God, and when we need to exert more effort?
- Study Philippians 2:12 – 13; 1 Corinthians 15:9 – 10; and Galatians 3:1 – 5. Create a simple but clear statement that summarizes the biblical theology of spiritual formation in your own words. Determine who does what in the changing of your heart and character.

## Chapter 3

# PICK YOUR WORD

*Where there is no prophetic vision*
*the people cast off restraint.*
— Proverbs 29:18 ESV

Most of us don't have any trouble coming up with a list of things we'd like to change about ourselves or the way we live. We could fill an entire page. College-ruled.

I used to make a list every January. Then I'd make a resolution for each area of my life—personal, relational, spiritual, health, financial, career. Like everyone else, by February I'd tried and failed on a couple of my resolutions. I gave up on others nearly from the start. And the rest had completely slipped my mind.

I felt frustrated. *What's the matter with me that I can't seem to make these changes?*

Then I started doing it differently. I decided to lose the long list of resolutions—all my sweeping promises to change—and zero in on just one word. One word for one whole year. That made all the difference. And I have full confidence it can work for you too.

This My One Word project is designed to channel your attention and effort with laserlike focus over an extended period of time. This is key to lasting change, and it will forge your character at a deep, sustainable level.

All you have to do is pick a word. But there's more to that process than you might imagine. So grab a sheet of paper, your journal, or write on the pages here, and I'll walk you through the process.

---

**INTEGRITY**

I am a radio personality, a writer, director, and producer. My one word is INTEGRITY. Integrity refers to the quality of a person's character at the core of their being. Integrity, for me, is one of the hardest words to live by, especially in the entertainment business. Striving for integrity reminds me to live by God's standards, not the media's. I want to live every day by my one word.

*—Sheila*

### *What Kind of Person Do You Want to Become?*

When considering changes we want to make, the tendency is to think in terms of specific behaviors. Typically, we give voice to our negative behaviors.

*I want to stop running late every day.*
*I need to stop overeating.*
*I want to stop looking at pornography online.*
*I'm tired of being disorganized.*
*I hate that I always say things I regret.*

Then, to formulate a resolution, we usually phrase it as a positive behavior.

*I'm going to manage my time better.*
*I'm going to eat healthier and lose weight.*
*I'll resist turning my computer on when I'm home alone.*

*I'm going to organize my entire house room by room.*
*I'm going to learn to bite my tongue.*

This is regret-based decision making. Regret can be a powerful motivator. Extremely powerful at times, depending on the severity of the consequences we've faced. But it's not always the best source of vision.

## *Vision, Not Regret*

We want to move forward with vision, not regret. Without vision, the Bible says in Proverbs 29:18, we tend to throw off restraint. We become unfocused and undisciplined. Regret doesn't stimulate forward-moving motion like vision does. And regret doesn't sustain the formation of new character the way that vision can. So we're going to craft a vision of the type of person we want to become this year.

Putting aside what you've done in the past, you're going to try something different. Instead of focusing on regrets and specific behaviors, I want you to spend some time with the question, Who do I really want to be? Or rather, *How* do I really want to be?

If you ask me who I want to be, I'm liable to blurt, "Eddie Van Halen!" I have a rock star fantasy. But that's not really how I want to be. I'd give you a vastly different answer if you asked me what kind of a person I want to become. I want to be a man of integrity, purity, and devotion.

So give this question some in-depth thought. Don't rush the process. Don't settle on the first word that comes to mind. My church and I take the better part of a month to choose the word we'll spend the rest of the year with.

Approach this patiently. An important part of the change process is allowing questions to remain questions for some period of time — so that truth can arise.

Spend a week or so reflecting on who you wish to become.

We tend to define ourselves by what we do. *I teach school. I'm a dentist. I own my own restaurant. I'm in college. I'm a surfer. I'm a soccer coach. I'm a single mom.* We tend to define who we want to be the same way. *I want to be the area's top realtor. I want to be married. I want to be a marathoner.*

This tendency is precisely why we need to dive deeper. Resist the pull to provide a surface-level answer to the penetrating question: Who do you want to become?

Consider the condition of your heart, your character, your soul. This requires a fierce commitment to being gut-honest with yourself. What you need is character formation, not to just stop doing this or start doing that.

Character formation and behavior modification isn't quite the same thing. Don't focus on the latter at the expense of the former. Our goal is not to live restrained but to effect true change. What we're after is a new normal that flows from the heart, not just amped-up willpower.

When we look beneath our behavior we discover what's driving it — the beliefs and motives that make up our character. The My One Word project is designed for character formation. Not just impulse control.

Our character is the mental and moral qualities distinctive to us — often referred to as our heart. The Bible teaches us to monitor and guard our hearts, explaining it's from here that our entire life flows. So what kind of person do you want to be at heart?

## *Identify Characteristics*

Do you want to get along better with your peers, your family, your boss, or your employees? What kind of person would get along with them? What characteristics would that person display?

Do you want to be more disciplined about how you live your life physically, spiritually, or financially? What kind of person would live a disciplined life? Describe that person. What drives them?

I think you get the idea. Don't just think about behaviors; think character and characteristics.

In a notebook or on a piece of paper, make a list of the characteristics of the person you want to become. In other words, describe the traits and motives of a person like that. Don't be intimidated into thinking, *I'll never be that way*. Just try to determine the kind of character required for you to live like you wish to live.

---

**TONE**

I manage a Christian women's recovery house. I lived a very hard lifestyle before coming to Christ, and it made me tougher than I care to be. I want to be a more sensitive and softer woman. I know that it's not what I say sometimes but how I say it. I want the recovery house to be a more comfortable environment for the women involved. My words and actions have a direct impact on that. I want to set the TONE.

—*Elizabeth*

## *Reduce and Define*

As you slowly gain a vision of the kind of person you want to become, you'll keep adding words and phrases to your list that capture the characteristics of that person. You might list nouns, adjectives, adverbs, or verbs—"being" words or "doing" words. Interestingly, we've found females tend to gravitate toward "being" words while males tend to pick "doing" words.

There is no wrong way to do this. Your list will be highly personal and unique. It may even contain words that only make sense to you.

My list usually includes words I like and words I don't feel excited about. I try not to self-edit the list as I come up with it. Deleting words off the list later is easy, plus it doesn't cost a dime to write them down. So fill a page if you need to.

Once you feel you've completed the listing process, pray, look over your list, and begin marking off all but ten or so of the words. Remove the ones that resonate the least with you. Don't worry about whether you "really need to work on that." If it doesn't resonate strongly with you right now, cross it out. Get your list down to ten words or less.

Once you have your short list, write a brief description of what those words mean to you. Look them up in the dictionary. Note their definitions. Look at their synonyms. And look them up in the Bible.

In this stage of the process you may find a related word you like better than the ones on your list — that's fine, write it down. You may also decide there's a word or two on there, after researching them, that you definitely don't want to choose. That's fine too — mark them off.

Pray. Ask God to guide you and give you clarity of thought and mind as you spend a few days thinking over your short list. Weigh each word and the implication it might have on your life. See if one of them manages to rise to the top. Ask God to bring one to the forefront.

## *Pick Your Word*

Now go ahead and pick your word from the list. Don't panic. This exercise is not about changing everything that needs to be changed but focusing and purposing to do something about one thing.

Seminary professor Howard Hendricks has said, "The secret to concentration is elimination." In order to concentrate on one thing, we're going to push others to the back burner for now. This is what we must to do to focus. Change is possible, but focus is required.

You might worry about picking the exact "right" word. Or picking the word "God intends" for you. Don't stress. If you went through the process outlined above, all of the words on your list are right for you.

### SHHH

I asked God for a word. For about four days, as I thought about it, my word was LIGHT. Safe. Doable. I thought God would be so proud that I chose such a wonderful word. After all, Jesus is the capital "L" light, and we should all be lowercase lights that point to him.

Good, except that tonight God did that thing he does every single time I ask him. He delivered. He delivered a word hand-picked for this child: SHHH.

SHHH means I don't have to verbalize every thought that is in my head at that moment.

SHHH means my quiet time in the morning is more about waiting on the gentle voice of my Savior than me spouting off a laundry list of my needs for the day.

SHHH means that there will be less opportunity for me to gossip, hurt someone's feelings, sound boastful or prideful. Less opportunity to sin.

Thanks, Dad, for delivering.

*—Rebecca*

If you zeroed in on character and motives in this exercise, you'll be pleased with any progress you make on any of the words on your list. And God is honored not by your chosen word but by your faith in him to effect change through this process.

So if you need more patience *and* more kindness *and* more love *and* more discipline in your life, but you pick LOVE and just become more loving this year — is that not a tremendous gain? Is that not success?

If you didn't pick LOVE but picked PATIENCE instead, and you focused on that for a year, my guess is you will grow more loving as you learn to be patient. Your word, whatever it is, will have farther-reaching effects than you can imagine now.

While I didn't want you to choose the first word that came to mind at the start of this process, I also don't want you paralyzed by the idea you'll somehow pick the wrong word. At this point you've thought, reflected, journaled, researched, and prayed. Now take a step of faith — pick one word. And choose a verse to go with it.

My one word is:

________________________________________

My verse is:

________________________________________

It is better to do something about one thing than nothing about everything. That is what this elimination process is about — that's what this whole project is about.

I am going to help you do something about this one thing this year. And I fully believe you'll be amazed at what you discover by engaging with your one word in the months ahead.

To the side, you'll see the top ten most-often-picked words in the My One Word movement according to our website (myoneword.org), where nearly five thousand people have posted their words. And in the coming chapters you'll learn how and why I chose some of my own one words. But first, there are few

### *TOP TEN MOST-OFTEN-PICKED WORDS*

1. Trust
2. Patience
3. Love
4. Discipline
5. Focus
6. Faith
7. Surrender
8. Peace
9. Listen
10. Joy

things you need to have in view to make this year successful with your word. So let's turn our attention to that next as I tell you about a couple guys I had coffee with once.

## *Reflect*

- What kind of person do you want to become this year?
- What drives your desire to be this kind of person?
- Describe the characteristics of this kind of person. Make a list of words based on this description.
- Reduce your list to ten words or less and research those words. Use the dictionary and your Bible, perhaps a thesaurus.
- Choose one word from your list to be your one word for this year.
- Also choose a Bible verse that speaks to you about your chosen word and memorize it. This will provide a foundation of truth you can continually return to and will fuel your hope to change.
- What initial expectations do you have regarding the impact of your word?

## Chapter 4

# SELF-DECEPTION

*Behold, You desire truth in the innermost being,*
*And in the hidden part You will make me know wisdom.*
— PSALM 51:6 NASB

There are a few things you need to have starting out on your My One Word journey. You'll keep touching base with them throughout the year too. They include an accurate view of who you are now, an accurate view of Christ, and an accurate view of who you are in Christ.

Let me explain with the story of a gentleman I had coffee with.

Jerry was older than myself. He had the look of an artist. Calloused hands revealed the nature of his work. Dark hair pulled into a low ponytail extended well below a hat. Not many men can pull off a beret-like hat, but Jerry wore it with ease.

His voice projected confidence as he spoke with the cadence of a poet. In fact, looking at him over my piping-hot cup of coffee, I thought, *This guy seems to be weathering life pretty well.*

The invitation for coffee originated with an email. He wanted to speak with the pastor regarding where "his gifts could best be used in a church like ours." Said he'd moved to Wilmington recently because "the Lord had called him here." Said he had lots of experience at his previous church that he thought could be valuable. And he wanted to get involved.

We began with the standard introductory chitchat. He was very complimentary of the church and my teaching. He'd come from a large church up north and thought he could help our church and people grow.

I was listening.

---

## MIRROR

Reflect. Reverse. Remember. I guess that is what my word MIRROR really encompasses.

*Reflect:* In all ways this year, I will strive to reflect the image of Christ.

*Reverse:* Like a reflection in a mirror—the image is in reverse. This year I want to do the reverse of how I would have normally reacted in situations where I have been less than Christlike.

*Remember:* I want to remember that when I speak, my words might say one thing but my expressions might say another, so I want to act as if I am speaking into a mirror, so my expressions are always kind in nature.

*—Jim*

---

Before I could ask him to tell me his story, he did. He told me of his life up north and the adventure of meeting and marrying the girl of his dreams. He told me about the money and his accomplishments. I didn't fully track with all he was saying and half-saying, but I got the sense that if I could track with it, I'd be impressed.

Then he switched gears to say how terrific his former church was and implied that "we" (our church) ought to be more like "them" (his old church). I nodded; I am always trying to learn.

Only, the more he talked the more vague he became. The less

clear, but the more spiritual sounding. As a pastor who has listened to a lot of people over a lot of cups of coffee, I know that spiritual language can be a great cover for the truth.

With my coffee cup now nearly empty, I asked my first question.

"Can you tell me more about your work?"

He told me of his life as an award-winning designer whose skills were in high demand. This led to other stories about how no one appreciated his talent. He mentioned there were not very many markets that could support the level of talent that the Lord had given him.

"Tell me about your wife," I interjected, wanting a fuller picture. I believe you can tell a lot about a man by how he speaks about his wife.

"We are knitted together," he assured me. Then he spoke of the romantic volatility that goes along with being married to a creative genius in high demand. The Lord had truly blessed him, he said, and his wife needed to be more appreciative of God's favor on him. He told me they'd been married for fifteen years and that she had recently moved to the southeast coast.

"*She* recently moved to the coast?" I inquired. I'm married and I have moved several times, but I would never say, "Julie moved." I'd say, "We moved."

"What brought her to the southeast coast?" I asked.

"The Lord," he answered. No elaboration.

"The Lord brought her here without you?" Again, partly as a question and partly asserting that this sounded a little off.

He paused, then said in a less-confident tone, "Well, the truth is we've had some issues. She's really frustrated with me. But ... she doesn't understand." He sighed.

Then he stated, "She left me."

Finally we were getting somewhere.

It turned out Jerry's wife had moved to get away from him. And he'd come here chasing her while telling himself and anyone who would listen that God had called him here with a certain (but unclear) plan.

## *Getting to the Truth*

I downed the last sip of my now-cold caramel-colored coffee and asked Jerry to tell me what was *really* going on in his life.

At this point he listed his problems very concisely: his marriage was empty, he was lonely, he felt far from God, and he was broke. Then he went into some detail.

He couldn't find satisfaction in his marriage, because his wife didn't understand or appreciate him enough. He couldn't find satisfaction in his job, because no one would pay him what he thought he was worth.

"I'm an artist. I do ministry through my art — but few people are able to see the value in that," he lamented. "I can't make a living doing what God has called me to do." And so he did much of nothing, and in his attempt to find his calling (aka his dream job), he'd run out of money.

Quickly upon admitting all this, Jerry reverted to spiritual-speak. He used Christian slogans and platitudes to spiff up the true condition of his life and heart. Next he trailed off on some spiritual tangents. It always amazes me how many people would rather debate whether or not Christians can raise someone from the dead than discuss how to live their own life with spiritual integrity and vitality.

Jerry came full circle, and we were soon back to how he felt he could help the body of believers at Port City Community Church. "So at my old church I was developing a program to help artistic men use their gifts to ..." Jerry talked at length about that before zeroing in on a Bible study they did that he believed I should take our whole church through. He explained how it addressed the core issues of every man: marriage, friendships, finances, and an intimate walk with Christ.

He concluded his five-star review of the study with the resounding assertion: "It changed my life!"

I was poised between my desire to do the easy thing — politely tell him I'd think about it and then get up to head back to the church — or do the hard thing and tell him the truth. I opted for the latter. He needed some truth in his innermost being. We all do.

I calmly recounted the conversation we'd just had. "Let me get this straight, Jerry. You just told me your marriage is a mess, you have no friends or money, and you feel far from God. Right?"

He slowly nodded.

"And then you told me about this extraordinary experience with a program that addresses the core needs of every man — marriage, friendship, finances, and faith — and how it absolutely changed your life." I sat back and held the moment, deciding how pointed to be.

"Your life has not changed," I announced. "Your marriage is worse. You have no money. You have no support network. You claim to be following God but you feel far from him, and your life is in shambles. And you are using spiritual language and knowledge of biblical stories and principles to avoid looking at that truth."

(Attention pastors, this is how *not* to get invited for more coffee.)

He was stunned. I suspect he had done a lot of mental gymnastics to avoid facing what I'd plainly laid out before him. The Bible says in Galatians 6:3 that if "anyone thinks he is something when he is nothing, he deceives himself" (NASB). I was holding up a mirror, hoping Jerry would see that he was self-deceived.

## KNOWLEDGE

Last year I heard about My One Word and decided to pray the word KNOWLEDGE over my life. I wanted to grasp God's Word, and I wanted to know him in a deeper way. God showed me so much about him, and even some things about myself—things I would rather not have seen but that were necessary for my growth.

God showed me things in my life that were not good for me. And things I was avoiding facing. Bringing these to light ultimately helped me know him deeper. I had to accept things in my life that only he could help me with in order to grow in him.

It was a life-changing year and God did miracles in my life. Things I had prayed over for years started happening. So in the midst of discovering the things I did not like in myself, he was also blessing me. You see, in order to know God, you have to know yourself. You have to see who you are and be willing to change into a vessel for him. That is when I truly learned to know him in a deeper way.

—*Kara*

### *Where Are You Now?*

You and I need to have an accurate picture of where we are now, today, in reference to our character and our one word. It does us no good to rosy things up with denial. We can't start out strong on this journey if we're starting out in the dark.

If I were to blindfold you, walk you through a day of life while holding your hand, and at the end of the day say, "Okay, go home," but didn't take off your blindfold, you'd have no idea which way to head. Even if you had a clear image of "home" in your mind. Even if you had a strong desire to be home. Odds are high you wouldn't make it to your destination.

We can't get from here to there with our one word if we are unwilling to take an honest look at where *here* is. No need to bring regret onto the scene. Just look objectively at where you are now; think about how you got here.

Look at the good and the bad. What areas of your life are you currently displaying the characteristics of your one word, and what areas are you not? What are the wise choices or the godly habits that have led to the good? And what are the foolish choices or the destructive habits that have led to the bad?

When we live too many days in the dark with our eyes closed to the truth — ignoring reality, ignoring God's corrective measures, ignoring the counsel of wise friends and the Bible — we inevitably wake up one day, look around, and think, *How did I get here? How did it come to this?*

Maybe that's where you're at now. The exercise of picking your one word helped you take stock of where you are in light of where you want or need to be. The distance between the two may be large right now. But don't panic, that is what the gospel of Christ is for. And that's why we spend a year with our one word.

### *Look Twice*

Having acknowledged where you've messed up or fallen short, you are now in the best possible position to move forward. The psalmist David illustrates this in Psalm 51:5–7: "Look, I was guilty of sin from birth, a sinner the moment my mother conceived me. Look, you desire integrity in the inner man; you want me to possess wisdom. Sprinkle me with water and I will be pure; wash me and I will be whiter than snow" (NET).

"Look," David says. *Behold*, he implores twice.

We have to look. We need to notice what the reality is. Our hearts need us to see it. Our spouses need us to see it. Our kids need us to see it. We cannot shut our eyes and refuse to see how we truly are.

"Look," David says. The reality is I am a sinner through and through. I am so prone to sin, it comes as natural as walking, as easy as breathing. We cannot think of ourselves as something when we are nothing. To lose sight of our true condition apart from God is to deceive ourselves. And to deceive ourselves is to stunt our own spiritual growth.

"Look," David says again. God desires truth in my innermost being. He expects integrity and wisdom to reside within me. The word *wisdom* here doesn't refer to learning. It's not about being well educated or well read. It's about moral insight. God wants his truth and his standards on the scene in our hearts.

David's two demands to look draw a stark contrast between who we are (sinners) and who we are called to be (morally sound). Between where we are today and the ideal God has for us. Our one word does that too.

Seeing this juxtaposition, David does the only thing any of us can do when the difference between who we are and who God calls us to become comes into view: he appeals to God, in verse seven, to transform him.

For this year with our one word to have the impact we desire, we must start with an accurate view of ourselves. Of our hearts, our tendencies, our motives, and where they are leading us. Then ask God to wash our innermost being in his grace and truth.

## *The Mirror*

Aside from having coffee with someone willing to be totally blunt with us, how do we gain an accurate view of ourselves? We look regularly in the mirror of God's Word.

The metaphor of the Bible as a mirror comes from the pen of James, who writes: "Do not merely listen to the word, and so deceive yourselves. Do what it says. Anyone who listens to the word but does not do what it says is like someone who looks at his face in a mirror and, after looking at himself, goes away and immediately forgets what he looks like. But whoever looks intently into the perfect law that gives freedom, and continues in it — not forgetting what they have heard, but doing it — they will be blessed in what they do" (James 1:22 – 25).

The best method of self-examination is looking into the mirror of God's Word — reading Scripture. Its sacred words have a way of laying our hearts open before our merciful God (Hebrews 4:12 – 13). The Bible is described as a God-breathed, living document able to teach us, rebuke us, and correct us (2 Timothy 3:16). It wasn't written for our information, but for our transformation.

Dallas Willard said, "Bible memorization is absolutely fundamental to spiritual formation. If I had to choose between all the disciplines of the spiritual life and take only one, I would choose Bible memorization."[5]

That's because, apart from the Word of God, we cannot know who God is and how God is. And apart from it, we don't readily recognize who or how we truly are either. And we don't see our potential in Christ.

Don't merely read verses; if that is all we do, we run the risk of deceiving ourselves. Don't just pile up biblical information in your head. Let it soak into your heart. Let it interpret you. And then let it seep out through your actions.

As long as we file the truth neatly into a "belief category," we will remain deceived. Only when we begin to let what we *believe* affect what we *do* are we able to embrace the process of formation.

Read that previous sentence again.

5 Dallas Willard, *The Great Omission: Rediscovering Jesus' Essential Teachings on Discipleship* (New York: HarperCollins, 2006), 58.

It's easy to read the Bible, nod our heads in agreement, and go on with our lives thinking we are changed because we "know" this stuff. As James points out, that's like seeing ourselves in a mirror and then walking away and forgetting what we look like. That's spiritual amnesia. *Applying* what the Bible says is the cure.

We can't just talk about our one word, why we picked it, and what we hope it will do for us; we have to *do* it, *apply* it. Spouting off long enough about something often deludes us into thinking we've addressed the issue.

Talk is too often substituted for action. Knowledge is too often mistaken for transformation. And we — you and me — are too often self-deceived.

Self-deception runs rampant. I see it frequently.

A middle-aged man comes up after a service and tells me he's been in church his whole life. Later in the conversation I learn he wasn't in church during college or after that while building his career. I correct him: "You went to church when you were young, and you have been *away* from the church your whole life."

A woman comes and tells me about her struggle to connect with her church small group. She tells me she's really trying but it won't work. I ask a couple of questions and learn she's been to small group twice in three months. I remind her, "You have to show up in order to connect. If you are not showing up, you are not trying."

A couple sits before me. "He drinks too much," she complains.

He retorts: "My drinking is not a problem. She blows it out of proportion. She's gotten so obsessed about it that I have to go to the garage and chug a beer when she's not looking in order to have a drink, or she'll nag me about it nonstop. She's the one with the problem."

I have to tell him, "Your drinking has landed you two here for counseling. I think it has officially become a problem."

Don't forget that when we stop allowing truth in, either because it's painful or unflattering or inconvenient, we will wind up self-deceived. Positive thinking is commendable but denial is detrimental.

### SUCCESS

I have spent my life believing that my successes are to my credit and my failures are my fault. Neither is true. My successes and failures are a product of God's work in my life. Jesus took the blame when he took my sins upon himself and died on the cross in my place. Jesus took the glory when he conquered the grave and resurrected. Therefore, the life I live is not my own. I have died with Christ and now live to glorify him. My past, present, and future belong to him. I am now released from the bondage of shame that stems from my failures. I am now released from the weight of my own pride, which would seek to take hold of success and claim it for my own selfish motives.

—*Tim*

## *Held Back*

Now it's time to note that not only are we plagued by a rosier view of ourselves than is accurate, but at times we're held back by a worse view of ourselves than is accurate.

Or at least by an incomplete view. That was Dan's problem.

"What do you *want* to do?" I asked the younger man sitting across from me, two coffee cups on the table between us. The question seemed like a logical place to start with someone struggling to figure out what to do with his life.

Dan hesitated. He sat there looking at me, blond hair resting on his shoulders, as if I'd just asked the oddest question he'd ever heard.

Dan struck me as a fun-loving guy who actually had his head on straight and his stuff together. I could see the potential in him. He should have had confidence, but he didn't.

I asked him to tell me his story. He told me of good parents, a good childhood, and the wrong friends. A common story.

Alcohol had become a part of his life at age sixteen. By twenty, it was his life. He told me this readily but hung his head as he said it. Shame over his past seemed to settle in the air around us.

But then Dan told me how he'd come to Christ, that he had forgiveness. That he'd sobered up. And that he'd come to our church, gotten involved, and started walking with God.

He sat across from me with four years of sobriety under his belt. He'd been dry just as long as he'd been a drunk. You would think the scales had finally been evened. You'd think he'd be planning his future as a man of God with his whole life in front of him. But he couldn't answer my question about what he would like to do now or next year or in the decades to come.

I tried a different line of questioning. "What do you think about every day when you get up?" I hoped to help him identify his God-given bent or passions. "What drives you?"

He sat there for a moment, wrapping his fingers around the paper coffee cup while trying to wrap his mind around my questions and their answers.

Finally he spoke. "I wake up every day and try not to drink."

"That's it?" I asked. "That drives you every day? All you think is *I won't drink*?"

He explained to me that he has to concentrate every day on trying not to drink because the same man will drink again.

I understand the nature of addiction. I've heard the high statistics on relapse. But I also know the power of vision. I firmly believe vision-fueled action is more powerful than regret-based restraint. And more than that, I know the power of the gospel, the gospel that saved Dan's soul.

So I asked Dan, "Are you the same man?"

Silence.

"Dan, when all we do is try *not* to do what we've always done in an attempt to keep from being what we've always been, the future goes unnoticed and unfulfilled. We walk into the future facing backwards, so afraid of what we've been that we never see what we actually are. Or where we can head *in Christ*."

I talked with him about 2 Corinthians 5:17, which promises, "Therefore, if anyone is in Christ, he is a new creation. The old has passed away; behold, the new has come" (ESV). This is another call to look—"Behold, you are now made new."

We talked about God having a plan for Dan's life when he'd created him in his mother's womb, a plan that extends beyond his daily mission of not drinking.

"What would you do if your drinking wasn't an issue?"

"I'd go to college. Maybe study business."

"Great. I think you can do that while staying sober. You are a new creature in Christ."

Dan's smile was full of possibilities.

He went to college that fall. And as far as I know, he's still clean and sober and on his way to a successful career.

Dan needed an accurate view of where he was right then, not a worse view. And he needed a view of who he is and where he is headed in Christ.

### *You Are New*

You may have struggled to change many times and resolved that you will always be the way you are. "It's just the way I am," you lament.

This is self-deception! Your lament is simply not true. You are a new creation in Christ, even if you aren't yet walking that out. So call on God, work out your salvation, and apply his Word to your thinking and actions (Philippians 2:12).

The truth is that God is at work in our innermost being, and he has promised to complete the work he's begun (Philippians

1:6). You and I are not yet what we shall be (1 John 3:4), but being in Christ changes everything.

Thinking of ourselves as more than we are can lead to self-deception. However, the opposite is true as well. To think we are *less* than we are in Christ is equally deceptive. In Christ, we are more than overcomers, more than conquerors (Romans 8:37; 1 Corinthians 15:57).

To recap, three things are required for your formation to happen this year with your one word:

1. An accurate view of Christ
2. An accurate view of yourself
3. An accurate view of yourself in Christ

Regularly looking into Scripture will help with all three. So will regularly looking through the lens of your one word.

More about that lens later, but for now let's talk in the following chapter about the next thing you need to do to begin your one-word journey.

### *Reflect*

- Do you tend to be more like Jerry or more like Dan in your view of yourself?
- Describe an accurate — not rosier and not worse — view of where you are now with regard to your one word. Then think about the choices, habits, and beliefs that got you here.
- Describe an accurate — if not fully here yet — view of where you are in Christ with reference to your one word. Search the Scriptures to help you answer this! Record God's promises.

## Chapter 5

# KEEP IT IN FRONT OF YOU

*These commandments that I give you today are to be on your hearts.... Tie them as symbols on your hands and bind them on your foreheads.*

— DEUTERONOMY 6:6, 8

He was turning blue.

*I think I've just killed the best kid in my youth group!*

That was the first thought to run through my head. The second?

*I am* so *getting fired for this!*

The job of a youth pastor hangs precariously on each game he chooses for the weekly youth group meetings. You need a fine blend of safety and risk. Humor is also a necessity, and a certain gross-factor is a major plus. But deviation too far in any one of these directions can land you in serious trouble.

I'd been convinced that this particular game struck the perfect balance of risk and fun. It was simple enough. Self-explanatory, I thought. Human bowling — we'd be bowling with humans. My youth group was *very* excited about this little adventure. As their new youth pastor, I was sure this would go down in youth group history, and it did.

My planning was impeccable. The execution, well, not quite so much.

We sang songs, did some Bible study, prayed for one another, and then it was time to bowl. I propped several eight-foot-long tables on their side end-to-end to form a "lane" in our makeshift bowling alley. I set up the pins about ten feet from the wall at the end of the lane. Then, about twenty feet from the pins, we'd launch our human-ball to knock 'em down!

Randy, a seventh grader (seventh graders make the best candidates for stuff like this), positioned himself as the human bowling ball by lying on his stomach on a skateboard, facing headfirst toward the pins. Because I valued both Randy and my job, he was wearing a helmet — safety first! — and his life was in the hands of my college-aged intern and his friend.

They would push Randy down the "alley" toward the pins, where he would knock down as many pins as possible with his head. As Randy broke through the pins, I'd be positioned in the ten-foot space between him and the wall, catching him by the shoulders. I'd bring him safely to a stop.

That was the idea anyway.

Unfortunately, while I was still assembling the rest of the group into the assigned spectator sections on either side of the lane, my overzealous intern and his friend counted, "One, two, three — go!"

Hearing the count, I turned just in time to see Randy zipping headfirst down the lane toward the pins. It looked like it was going to be a strike.

Before I could yell "wait," Randy sailed right through the pins, knocking them all down. He sailed right through the unmanned ten-foot safety zone, then right into the wall at the end of the lane. *Bam!* Randy's head disappeared inside the wall, sending pieces of wallboard and insulation flying.

I rushed to the scene to find Randy's body jutting out from the wall like the Wicked Witch of the East under Dorothy's house. We moved the skateboard, then carefully unwedged Randy's head. The impact had jammed the helmet down over the back of his skull. The chin strap stretched tight across his neck, cutting off his oxygen.

He was turning blue, and I was turning pale.

After working Randy free from the helmet's grip, we helped him outside for some fresh air. His color reverted to normal.

"I think I'm okay," he finally said, clearly shaken.

With my first fear alleviated, my second kicked in strong. Randy had survived but would my career? I envisioned sitting in a future interview for another youth pastor position, being asked to explain why I was fired from the last church.

Turns out, Randy and I both survived. Randy continued to mature at that church, and fortunately so did I. But it was a lesson I would not forget; I *couldn't* forget if I tried. Each time I walked into the youth group room, I saw a giant head-sized hole in the wall. It served as a reminder, keeping the near-disaster ever before me.

Maybe that's why the deacons never had the hole fixed.

## *Keep It before You*

Reality is, we seldom need reminders about the dumb things we've done. They haunt us, inserting themselves into our thoughts. Rarely do we need help remembering our regrets or recognizing the fact that we are not who we want to be.

We don't just notice the "holes" in our walls; we fixate on them, letting them define us. While they might motivate us to change, they also load us down with a measure of guilt. That's why, instead of choosing our one word by looking at who we are, we choose our one word with a forward-facing vision of who we want to *become* in the future.

Your task now is to keep your word in front of you daily. Take your eyes off the mistakes, the regrets, the failures — the gap between where you are and where you want to be — and focus on the one thing you want God to do in you this year. Focus on your one word.

---

### UNCHAINED

My past mistakes no longer define me. I am UNCHAINED.

*—Cassidy*

---

Every year I keep my one word in front of me daily. For instance, the year my word was FINISH I wrote it on a notecard and stuck it on my dashboard. I saw it at the start of my day when I left for work, midday if I left for lunch, and again on my way home. I saw FINISH when running errands, visiting people at the hospital, or fastening my board to the roof rack to hit the beach. It stayed in front of me.

Part of my chosen discipline that year included reading several books start-to-finish. So I kept the stack of selected reading sitting in front of me on my desk. The books served as pointed reminders, helping me stay focused on FINISH, as well as reminding me that, like the books themselves with their dog-eared pages, I'm a work in progress.

A gentleman in our church sometimes engraves my words onto wooden plaques for me. I hang those in my office. At this moment, to my right, below the picture of a pelican soaring over the surf, hangs a dark brown plaque with the word KNOWL-

EDGE skillfully carved into the grain. Underneath it hangs another wood plaque with the word AFFECT.

I hear from people engaged in the My One Word movement, and I'm always fascinated to learn how they keep their words in front of them. They tell me they've typed them into screen savers or stamped them onto jewelry. They've written them in their Twitter bios and on their bathroom mirrors. They've made it a repeating all-day event on their iPhone calendars. Some even find a theme song with their one word in it.

You could have a T-shirt or key chain made with your one word. A stepping stone for your garden or a scrapbook. You can stencil it on your wall, painting over it next year or adding to it with your next one word. The idea is just to keep it before you this year so you won't forget — or you *will* forget. There is a reason the phrase "Out of sight, out of mind" is cliché.

> I write my word on an index card and place it in a visible spot like the visor of my car or the junk drawer in our kitchen. I know that last one sounds funny, but that drawer contains odds and ends that I need throughout the day every day.
>
> —*Holly*

My word stays in front of me, serving as a reminder, urging me to focus and trust the process. Sometimes it alerts me to pay closer attention. Sometimes it calls me to look at things differently. Other times it assures me I'm making progress. Whether life is going well or I've recently blown it, the sight of my word rekindles my faith that God will continue to shape and form my character, for my sake and his.

I just have to remember it.

## *Remember to Remember*

The year was drawing to a close. Richard and Julia were discussing the twelve months past. As empty nesters they rejoiced in how well their kids were doing. They talked about the condition of their marriage and shared their hopes for the coming year.

Julia asked Richard how his one word affected him that year.

"My word really impacted me in the early part of the year," Richard said, "but lately it's not been as powerful." He paused, then added, "In fact, I can't even remember now what my word is."

Julia laughed. "I know we are getting to the age when things slip the memory, but Richard, your one word is REMEMBER!"

Richard failed to remember REMEMBER.

You and I are just as recall-challenged. Forgetfulness isn't just a problem for Richard; it's a problem for us all. Who among us hasn't put a sticky note in a prominent place or emailed ourselves a reminder in order to recall something important?

Life is full. We're busy. We become distracted. Then, preoccupied, we forget.

This is not a new challenge either. In the days of Moses, the people of God were charged with remembering one main thing: "Hear, O Israel: the LORD our God, the LORD is one" (Deuteronomy 6:4). This was a declaration of their faith and their allegiance to the one true God. It was followed by the command to love God with all their heart, soul, and strength.

This command seems simple enough, easy to remember. Yet, like us, the Israelites all-too-easily forgot things they fully intended to remember. With the invention of Post-it notes far off in the future, they'd have scribes write the passages out on little pieces of papyrus. Then they'd shove the reminders into little boxes called *tefillin* and strap the boxes to their arms or foreheads. They kept the words of the command before them—literally.

It is quite hard to forget something that is strapped to your forehead. I am not suggesting that you put your one word in a box and attach it to your head, but it would be better than forgetting it.

## SPONGEBOB

Before anyone thinks I didn't take this seriously, let me explain. Last year was the worst year of my life in the professional sense. We risked everything we owned in a dream that didn't work out the way we hoped, and I fell into a woe-is-me mind-set. I had to take a job delivering pizzas until we could get our new business started. I felt embarrassed and that I deserved better. Then one day, I was watching *SpongeBob SquarePants*, and it dawned on me: this guy has it right. He loves his job (he's a fry cook, for the SpongeBob-impaired among us), and he treats everyone like they're his best friend—even Squidward, who dislikes him. He's always in a good mood and wants to share a smile with everyone. Every bad situation he and his sidekick Patrick get in, they make the best of it and have fun doing it. That's the way I want to be: happy, forgiving, and fun to be around. Like SpongeBob SquarePants.

—*Chris*

### *Fully Enjoy Your Word*

A group of us sat in my office talking about our year's experience with My One Word. We recalled the excitement with which we'd narrowed down our list of words eleven months earlier and picked just one. We talked about the energy with which we'd begun the year with our word. Everyone had come out of the gate with a bang!

My friend and Rachel's husband, Rick, talked about the word he'd selected that year. He prayerfully settled on the word ENJOY while running on the beach one sunny January morning (it's nice living in the South). He said he felt God had let him pick the best word ever. *This was going to be a great year!*

He would learn to enjoy his family more, enjoy his meals more, enjoy his hobbies more, enjoy nature more, and enjoy his work more. He told us the prospect of an entire year to look through the lens of enjoyment brought a sense of excitement, fusing each day with fresh anticipation.

> I always print my word and frame it, then put it somewhere in my home where I'll see it often. I also post it on the wall right above my computer at work. Literally keeping my word in front of my face is a great way for me to be constantly cognizant of applying it in my life.
>
> —*Emily*

Rick also said God used this word the first few weeks in a powerful way. Keeping his mind tuned to the word ENJOY, he found this quote by the Greek scholar Aristotle: "To enjoy the things we ought and to hate the things we ought has the greatest bearing on excellence of character."

His word began to expand into something more, taking on new depths of meaning. ENJOY would shape Rick's character in unexpected ways. Not only would Rick enjoy God's blessings that year; he would learn to align his standards of enjoyment with God's as well.

It was so cool hearing Rick recount all that ENJOY had done in just his first couple of months with the word. We waited for him to continue sharing his experiences with this incredible word. But he fell silent.

After a moment, Rick said he'd allowed the pace of his life and the things required of him personally and professionally to pull his attention away from his One Word project. After the first few months, he forgot to stay intentional about his word, and then he forgot it altogether. Rick's voice held a mixture of disbelief and regret. He looked around at each of us and announced, "I forgot to ENJOY this year!"

What gets noticed and measured gets done. And what gets ignored gets, well, ignored.

Talking together as a group that day, we concluded the single most difficult part of this One Word journey is continuing to focus on our word for a full year. To get the most out of this project, it's imperative that we find ways to regularly pay attention to it.

---

## DISCIPLINE

I chose the word DISCIPLINE, because I need to apply discipline to all areas of my life. I actually chose this word last year but was not disciplined enough to follow through and make it part of my life. So this year I am going to put the word everywhere, so it will remind me of the discipline I need to move forward in my life. I need more discipline to pray, to study, to work, to exercise, to meditate, etc. Every area of my life will benefit if I allow God to discipline me and if I practice discipline daily. I feel that by putting my one word out to the world, it will help me be more accountable and (dare I say it?) more disciplined!

—*Gretchen*

### *Don't Miss Out*

Seventeen years have passed since Randy's head rammed through that wall. He called me a few months ago wanting to tell me what God is doing in his life. He's married and working—*wait for it*—as a church youth pastor. Oh, and he assured me that his head is truly okay.

Randy also said the story of my human bowling fiasco is still making the rounds in certain circuits of youth pastors. Fortunately, it has grown to the status of lore without my name attached. I am glad that hole in the wall did not define Randy's life and equally thankful it did not define mine.

All of us have reminders of the things we wish we'd done differently—our holes in the wall. If we don't proactively keep our word in mind, we'll forget it and revert to staring at the holes, reliving our regrets.

Keep your word in front of you. Tape it to your mirror or dashboard. Make it your computer password. Write it into your social media bio. Tweet it once a week. Make it your Facebook status. Bind it to your forehead if necessary.

Don't fail to remember. That's your first challenge.

In the next chapter I'll explain the second challenge you'll face in your quest to let this one word change your life.

Don't stop short of all God can do in you this year through your word. Don't miss out, simply because you forgot! Change is possible, but focus is required.

Nail a sign engraved with your one word over the hole in your wall and press on toward a future made possible by God. And watch him transform your life in the coming year!

## *Reflect*

- Devise multiple ways to keep your word in front of you this year. Perhaps place your word in your home and in your car, on your computer, or at your desk.
- Are you on Facebook, Twitter, Pinterest, or other social media sites? Make your one word your status update. Add it to your profile descriptions. Make it your profile pic. Announce it to your followers and give them permission to periodically ask you how your one word is going.
- Spread the word about My One Word and your chosen word! The more your friends and family participate in this movement, the more your tribe will talk about it, and the more it will be brought to your mind.
- Go to www.myoneword.org, post your word and opt in for helpful reminders from us to focus on your word.

## Chapter 6

# HEARING ISN'T THE HARD PART

*"My sheep hear my voice,*
*and I know them, and they follow me."*
— John 10:27 ESV

We named him Meshach. That turned out to be prophetic, because he refused to bow down to the command of another.

Problem was, this wasn't the gutsy friend of Daniel found in the Old Testament, bucking the demands of a pagan king. This was my black Labrador retriever.

He came to me at eight weeks old, small and cute. A gift. Who wouldn't want a cuddly ball of black fur? His paws were three times the size of his head. That's a clue I missed. While he was clomping around the house chasing a racquet ball on paws the size of my own head, I didn't think about what might happen when he grew into those feet.

Didn't take long, however, to realize Meshach would not be an inside dog. Despite our commands against it, he'd climb onto our tile-topped kitchen table while we were gone. He liked the coolness of the tile on his tummy. But then he couldn't get down — with every try, his paws would slide out from under him on the smooth tiles. He'd be trapped on the table all day until we returned home from work.

There are not enough Clorox wipes for that.

On days we were home, he'd wait for us as we poured our coffee and then opened the fridge for some cream. Then he'd pounce on the unattended cup, spilling and drinking the coffee. It's terribly frustrating to have to fight your dog for the last cup of French roast.

If you are imagining a black lab with coffee breath, don't. Because the only thing Meshach liked more than coffee was the taste of toothpaste. If we left a tube on the bathroom counter, he'd find it, split it open, and lick every last bit of gel from inside. Plastic toothpaste carcasses littered our house.

---

### HEEL

This command tells a dog to get in the right place. It's a place of obedience, discipline, following, and servitude. It's not pulling the leash trying to get out in front, and it's not lagging behind, resisting the master's lead. I find myself needing to get back into my proper place—alongside Jesus, being humble, trusting, obedient, disciplined, and serving. "He has told you, O man, what is good; and what does the LORD require of you but to do justice, to love kindness, and to walk humbly with your God?" (Micah 6:8 NASB).

*—Thomas*

---

Then there was the time he chewed a large hole right through the middle of the drywall in our living room. I don't know how he did it, but I figured this wasn't good for his health. And I knew it wasn't good for mine.

So I set out to build a fence around our backyard and create a domain in which Meshach could reign — away from tile tables, caffeine, and tartar-control toothpaste. I figured a dog with a name like Meshach deserved a wooden picket fence; no chain-link fence would do. Besides, our homeowner association banned chain-link fences (a lesson I learned after I began erecting a chain-link fence).

As a youth pastor on a budget, I could not afford to purchase all the lumber at once, so I spread out the cost. First I purchased posts and concrete. I spent a weekend digging, setting, and leveling the posts that would support the boundaries of Meshach's kingdom.

Then I purchased the supporting lumber that would frame the sections of the fence. For weeks, I measured, sawed, and drove the frames into place. The final step was attaching the pickets to the frame. I'd buy as many pickets as I could afford in a week — maybe twenty or thirty at a time — and install them that weekend.

The whole process took about three months. Meshach hung out alongside me in the backyard, observing the construction of his fence. When construction began, he was twenty pounds of playful energy. In order to contain him before the fence was complete, I purchased a twenty-five-foot chain and connected one end to his collar and the other end to a small cinder block.

*There, that should secure him while I work.*

After just a week, it took a full-size cinder block to anchor him in the yard. Soon, he required two cinder blocks. By the end of the construction process, my young dog was strolling around my yard dragging three cinder blocks. Effortlessly.

Meshach emerged to the cinder-block-free freedom of his fully fenced-in backyard as a one-hundred-pound black brute of a dog. He could pull his own body weight without panting. I'd inadvertently given him the canine version of P90X.

Turns out Meshach did not appreciate the limited freedom his fence provided. The lure of what happens on the other side of it proved too much for him to ignore. So instead of staying where he belonged, he dug his way out.

I roamed the neighborhood in search of him, whistling and calling his name. He heard me but wouldn't come. Eventually I caught him, returned him to the yard, and filled in the hole he'd dug — only to have him dig his way out again as soon as I was gone.

This digging, calling, catching, filling the holes routine continued for weeks until a friend helped me install an invisible electrical fence. We buried a wire cable carrying an electrical charge around the perimeter of my yard. Meshach was fitted with a special collar that would deliver a safe, small shock as he got close to the wire, teaching him the boundaries in which he was intended to live.

Did it work? Yes, it worked great — as a personal backscratcher for Meshach. He'd back up to the invisible fence, lean his body into contact with the fence plane, and then treat the shock like some sort of massage. Once done with his back rub, he'd dig his way out and take off again, ignoring my commands.

"Meshach, stop! No … wait … Meshach, get away from that fence! Meshach … come back here!"

This went on for two years. I even took him to obedience school where he was hands down the least-behaved dog there. We worked really hard on teaching him the simple one-word commands "come" and "stay." Part of him wanted to obey; I could see it. But a larger part of him was easily distracted and wanted to play.

We were prime candidates for *Dog Whisperer*.

To my surprise, Meshach won the "most improved" award at the end of the ten weeks of obedience school. I thought he was finally maturing, but once school let out, Meshach stopped obeying his one-word commands. He'd only do what I asked to get a doggie treat. The rest of the time, he pretended not to hear me.

He heard me all right. He just refused to obey. Sounds like us with God sometimes, doesn't it? Jesus diagnosed us when he said "though hearing, they do not hear" (Matthew 13:13).

---

**MOTION**

---

I listen a lot, but I don't always do what I hear. I want to put action to what I hear from God and do what he wants me to do. So my one word is MOTION.

*—Thomas*

## *Hearing Is Obeying*

Everyone wants to know how they can hear God speaking to them. It's a question Rachel and I both get asked all the time.

According to Jesus, we shouldn't doubt that he speaks to us or doubt our ability to hear him. In John 10:27, he said, "My sheep hear my voice" (ESV). Those who belong to God, hear him speak.

Before you start to wonder if you truly belong to him because you're not sure you're hearing him speak, think about where you've been already in this exercise.

As you worked through the process of picking your word, you engaged in listening for God's direction. You prayed and asked what kind of person he wants you to become. You looked up verses containing your word. And you felt confirmation that this was to be your word. You do hear the voice of the Good Shepherd; the question is, will you follow his lead this year through this word?

Here's the thing: according to the Bible, God expects action to accompany our hearing. The two are linked. In the original language — in the Greek and Hebrew — they are linked. We are to obey what we read in Scripture and what we sense God whispering to our hearts. If we don't obey, we didn't really hear — though hearing, we did not hear, Jesus would say.

The category for hearing and not acting is called disobedience.

As a parent, I see the connection between hearing and doing. Last night my youngest asked me to give her a pedicure — at 9:30 p.m. I am certain this was a bedtime stall technique. Nevertheless, I painted her cute toes with crackle paint. After the final coat dried, I sent her off to bed.

This morning as we were cleaning the house, I asked her to put away the nail polish: "Please remove the nail polish from the coffee table and return it to its proper place in your bathroom."

After I'd finished cleaning the kitchen, I returned to the living room and noticed the pedicure kit still on the coffee table. My question to her was, "Hey, little bud, did you hear me?"

I didn't inquire about her desire to obey — when you are the authority, obedience is implied. It's expected. It's not up for negotiation or dismissal.

Once we've gotten a vision for our character, a word to focus on, and an obvious next step to take regarding our word, the challenge is to stop making excuses for inactivity. Stop pretending we can't yet proceed. And instead, obey.

Your word is chosen. You've committed to it. You are keeping it in front of you. Now obey from the heart. The apostle Paul writes, "But thanks be to God that though you were slaves to sin, you became obedient from the heart to that form of teaching to which you were committed" (Romans 6:17 NASB).

God will speak through the word you've committed to. But he doesn't speak just to be heard, he speaks to be followed and obeyed from the heart.

## *To Obey Is to Trust*

My friend and coauthor Rachel learned to obey from the heart the year she picked PERIPETY as her word. I know, who has heard of that? As a bunch of us sat in my office that February, each sharing our word and why we chose it, Rachel had to define hers for us. She's a communication instructor at the university and a self-professed word geek.

*Peripety*, according to Rachel, is a literary term that means the pivot point in the story where fortunes are reversed. "I learned it from Beth Moore," she said in defense when we all looked baffled by her choice. "Jesus is the ultimate peripety," she added. "The cross is the pivot point in history where our fortunes are reversed."

I thought that was pretty cool, but I wasn't sure how God would use a word like *peripety*.

But he did. I'll let Rachel tell you about it in her own words.

### Rachel Olsen and PERIPETY

The year I chose PERIPETY as my one word, I wasn't teaching at the university. My speaking schedule was light. And my only steady paycheck came from some work I did for a nonprofit group each month. Within weeks of settling on PERIPETY, my boss at the nonprofit told me they wanted me to take three months off from the job.

*Did they just say take three months off?* I asked myself. *Why?*

I was stunned. I loved doing this job. Rarely am I rendered speechless, but in that moment I was silent, confused.

My boss continued: "Rachel, during the next three months, we want you to question your calling to this job. We know you were called to it years ago when you started, but we want to make sure you are still called and still passionate about it. So you will take three months to think and pray about that. We'll continue paying you during the three months. At the end of three months, we want you to come tell us if you want your job back. At that point we'll discuss it."

*Three months with pay, but no clear guarantee of a job after that? Is this just a weird way of firing me or laying me off?* That's exactly what you'd be thinking too, right?

"So what do you think?" they asked.

"Do I have a choice?"

"No. You don't."

"Will I definitely have my job back in three months?"

"We will discuss it then. We don't have anyone lined up to replace you; we're not even sure how we're going to get the work covered during your three-month absence. But for now, you need to see if you even want your job back."

A long pause.

"And if you really want your job back, we will work it out and discuss what that will look like then."

I already knew I wanted my job back. I loved this job. I didn't want to lay it down — not for three months and certainly not for good. Besides, it provided my only steady year-round paycheck. I didn't just want this job; I relied on it.

"Go work on your next book," they said. "And we'll talk about this in three months."

I walked away shocked, confused, angry, and hurt. There wasn't enough chocolate in the house to handle that combination of emotions.

For weeks I peppered God with my questions. *Why is this happening? I don't need three months to decide if I want my job or not. I already know I do. Do you not want me to continue in this job? Did I do something wrong? Lord, what is going on and what am I supposed to do?*

There was relative silence from God in response to my questions, except for the word PERIPETY. That's all that would come to mind: a major pivot point in the story. A change in the course of events. A reversal of fortunes.

I knew what he was saying. I didn't like it or understand it, but I knew. And I knew what it meant I'd have to do. At the end of the three months, I told my boss I would not return to my job.

Immediately after giving up my only steady income, a series of things started to break. Big things. First my car and then my husband's car—to the tune of $1,600 in repairs. Then my cell phone died, and days later my daughter dropped hers and broke it. We were both still under contract—no new free phones for us. Next our home's AC unit died; it was July. That was $5,000 to replace. Oh, and our refrigerator died as well.

Inside of four weeks of laying down my only steady job, we incurred over $10,000 in unexpected expenses.

This worried my daughter. As I tucked her in one evening I could see she was stressed. She wouldn't tell me what the matter was, but God clued me in. "Honey, are you worried about our finances?" I asked.

"Yes," she admitted, water pooling in her young hazel eyes. "Can you get your job back, Mom?"

"Well, honey, I probably could. But I didn't give up the job because we had plenty of money. I gave it up because I believed that's what God wanted me to do. So I'm not going to try to get the job back because of these expenses. God would have to tell me to return to the job."

She didn't find much comfort in that answer. So I told her, "You know, Alaina, everyone tries to create a life for themselves that is worry-free. We want to earn enough money that we'll never have to worry about expenses, that we can always pay our bills and have money left to buy the things we want. We want job security and good health and problem-free days. We want to be in control and not have to rely on anyone to get our needs met, including God.

"But here's the deal, honey. If you can always manage your life yourself and solve all your own problems, you won't feel much need for God. You'll still have need for God, you just won't feel it. The life that everyone wants is really a life that doesn't require any faith. The Bible says that without faith, it is impossible to please God. So if you and I want to be people that please God, we're going to have to live a life that requires some faith.

"Big problems," I told her, "are really just big opportunities to trust God boldly and please him as we do. And big opportunities to trust God boldly don't come around every day. So let's pray and trust him to provide for us in this. I don't know how, but I believe he will take care of us."

She went to sleep that night in peace.

A week or so later, a stranger placed a $100 bill in my palm as they shook my hand. I assumed it was a note or business card until they walked away and I looked down.

At a speaking engagement that month, a woman purchased a couple of copies of my book and wrote her check for $500. The memo line said, "A love gift for you." I was astounded.

A few weeks later, a check for $1,000 arrived in the mail from someone I once attended church with. Her enclosed note said God had prompted her to take this out of her retirement account and send it to me. She said she'd resisted at first, not wanting to part with the cash, but ultimately decided she wanted to obey God more.

I showed the $100 bill to Alaina. I also showed her the two checks. We pulled the addresses off the two checks and sent thank-you cards. Before signing her name, Alaina wrote, "Thank you for showing me God can be trusted to provide." To Alaina, these amazing acts of unsolicited kindness proved God responds to trust and faith.

To me these experiences spoke of PERIPETY. And in one final major pivot of events at the end of that year, I received a new job that offered more income than the one I'd given up in blind obedience to God and my one word. My year with PERIPETY was a roller-coaster ride, but well worth the trip.

■ ■ ■

God spoke to Rachel through her one word. He used her word to guide her and to gain her trust in difficult circumstances. But she had to listen and obey.

God will speak to you through your one word too. You might think your biggest challenge will be to hear him speak, but it won't. Your biggest challenge will be to obey what you hear. Don't be like my Labrador, Meshach. Be like Meshach, the friend of Daniel who had the guts to trust and obey God, no matter the outcome.

**EXCUSELESS**

I am the queen of good intentions. Life takes a toll and it doesn't get done. This year ... no excuses.

*—Catherine*

### *Hearing God*

We obey from the heart because we trust what we hear. So it does start with hearing him. Since I'm frequently asked, "Mike, how do you know you're hearing from God?" let me give you the four ways I test it:

1. *Hearing God requires consistency in my walk.* The more disconnected I become from God, the harder it is for me to sense his lead. The first thing I look at is how consistent I've been lately. I believe God speaks to me not just to give me orders but out of love. He is not a genie or a tour guide, but my Father. Therefore, I talk with him regularly, not simply when I need directions or help. If you spend time with God daily, you will learn to recognize his voice and stay attuned to his lead.

   Ask yourself, "How consistent have I been lately in seeking God and abiding with him?"

2. *Hearing God requires clarity on his purpose.* God's directions for me always line up with his purposes. And his purposes always involve forming me into his image. My One Word is a great tool for discerning God's purposes for us in a given season. You have chosen your word based on what you believe God wants to do in you this year, so consider that his purpose for now. The greater clarity you have regarding his purposes, the easier it will be to understand his voice and follow.

   Ask yourself, "Does this line up with what I understand of God's purposes for me?"

3. *Hearing God requires confirmation in the Word.* I study the Scriptures daily with a submissive heart and a willingness to obey what is there, not to just find a verse to back up what I want to do. God will never direct us to do something that contradicts the teaching of the Bible. His Word will speak to you, either to confirm what you are sensing or to redirect you. Pay close attention to what you hear when you read it.

   Ask yourself, "Does this line up with what the whole of Scripture teaches?"

4. *Hearing God requires counsel from wise friends.* God's direction is frequently affirmed by those around me who know and love me. Notice I said *wise* friends. We all have people who will tell us what we want to hear. Wise counsel helps me see what I can't see from my own perspective. Surround yourself with wise friends who love God and you enough to tell you the truth.

   Ask yourself, "What have my friends and mentors advised?"

---

**STAND**

---

After overcoming my drug addiction, I decided to give up cigarettes too. On January 1, I had my last cigarette after twenty years of smoking. Recently I've been going through a fiery trial ... something that in the past would have sent me deep into a drug binge and depression. But praise God, he has given me the strength and hope to STAND in him! I'm standing with a smile, knowing that I have his love.

—*Lynn*

## *The Real Challenge*

About three years after bringing that little black ball of fur home, I heard a woman on the other side of my fence chasing after her dog in the ravine behind my house. She yelled repeatedly for him to come. The dog wasn't listening. Or rather, he was hearing her but not obeying.

In hopes of offering some comfort through commiseration I hollered, "My dog used to do the same thing."

"What did you do?" she asked, looking for some wisdom.

"I gave him away!"

It's true. After building multiple fences and subfences; after taking my wife to the dentist because Meshach broke her tooth; after replacing the chewed-up shoes, kids' toys, and toothpaste tubes; and after retrieving him from inside a neighbor's house where he was drinking out of their toilet, I found Meshach a good home with plenty of companionship and room to roam. He became the official dog of a college fraternity house!

God will speak through your word in the coming year. You'll hear his call to take new steps of faith. You'll hear his whispers of affection and direction. You'll hear his loving correction, and you'll hear his gentle reminders to persevere.

Your obedience will keep the lines of dialog open between you and God. God gives us insight or direction and then we respond with action. He follows up with further insight or an assignment. When we fail to respond with obedience, it may seem to us that God has stopped speaking. He hasn't; he is waiting for us to obey.

What if you hear God and he says something unexpected? Or he gives you a difficult task — or even a difficult year — with your one word? I'll address this in the next chapter and let my wife tell you about one of her one words.

The challenge will not be whether you hear him this year but whether you obey. Let your one word be a reminder to submit.

### *Reflect*

- What have you heard God say to you? Go through my list of four criteria above and test it.
- What next step has God revealed regarding your one word? If you don't know, pray and ask him to show you the next step. Think about the key verse you selected for your one word and let it guide you.
- State your next step as a declaration of intention and faith. Here is an example from my own life and my current one word, INVEST:

My next step based on INVEST is to start a mentoring group of young ministers to invest in.

The key verse I've selected comes from the parable of the talents in Matthew 25:26–27 (ESV) [italics for emphasis]:

> "But his master answered him, 'You wicked and slothful servant! You knew that I reap where I have not sown and gather where I scattered no seed? Then you ought to have *invested* my money with the bankers, and at my coming I should have received what was my own with interest.'"

The idea is that God has trusted me with skills and gifts that belong to him, and I will give an account to him for how I use them. This verse makes it clear that God expects an investment and a return on that. He expects me to risk what he's given me. As I look into my own life, I've often shied away from using my gifts, beyond the Sunday morning stage, to invest in others. I assume those on my staff and those who look to me for leadership are being developed instead of taking responsibility to sow what God has taught me into their lives. So based on what I know about God—he is not exacting and demanding, but generous and faithful—I will take what I've been given and intentionally INVEST it in others for the sake of a kingdom return.

My declaration is I am trusting that God will take what I invest, bless it, and it will yield a return in places that I have not sown nor gathered. Their families and ministries will benefit, because I trusted God's call to INVEST in others.

Chapter 7

# LET IT MORPH

*In their hearts humans plan their course,*
*but the* Lord *establishes their steps.*
— Proverbs 16:9

These pages are filled with examples of real people, the words they chose, and their reasons for picking them. Don't skip over these — I think you'll be inspired by their stories and learn from them.

Each of us has our reasons for picking our particular one word. Maybe you chose a word that will urge you to address a place of weakness. Or perhaps you chose one that will maximize an area of your strengths.

Maybe you chose a word you feel will direct your heart toward God. Or perhaps you chose one you hope will characterize your year ahead.

Regardless of what your one word is or why you chose it, God may have different or additional plans for you. He may do more with it than you imagined. That doesn't mean you have the wrong word or that you need to pick a new word; it's just a reminder to stay open to his lead.

Sometimes our one word turns out to be a prophetic statement about our year. I hear stories of this all the time. Someone chose the word X and X happened. But I also hear lots of stories with a different bent. Someone picked a word, imagining one thing, and the unexpected happened.

It's important to understand that we cannot obligate God in any way by the one word we choose. This is not a "name it and claim it" exercise. Nonetheless, God will work through your one word according to his purposes and for your maturity.

For example, I can't choose the word WEALTH and thereby force God to bring me lots of money in the coming year. But God will use that word and that year to teach me something about wealth; he will speak through my one word.

He might teach me the difference between earthly riches and spiritual riches. Or teach me about my inheritance in Christ. He might teach me not to put my trust in wealth. Or he might ask me to give my wealth away. The challenge, as we've established, will be for me to hear and obey what God is saying through this word.

If we expect our word to be a prophetic proclamation about our year ahead — either because we felt God lead us to the word or because we want so badly for it to be so — we might be surprised at the outcome.

### REFLECT

This year my word is REFLECT. I wanted a word that would help me be more consistent in reflecting on God's Word with quiet times, prayer, and journaling, and this seemed like the perfect fit. Then while I was standing in front of a mirror I had an ah-ha moment. I realized that my word could also mean to reflect God's image in this world more effectively. That is when I realized I had found my word.

*—Chris*

## *Unexpected Joy*

Fiction writer Marybeth Whalen realized this the year she chose the word JOY. I'll let her tell you how that went.

### Marybeth Whalen and JOY

JOY. My word for the year came to me with a certainty that left no room for any other choice. I knew it was right. A friend even sent me a Christmas ornament with the word written in silver, swirly, fancy letters the same week I selected it. A confirmation!

I hung the ornament from my kitchen window so I would see it every day, a reminder of all the joy that would be coming my way. I was thankful that God had directed me to such a wonderful word. It felt like a promise.

One year later, I can tell you even the most innocuous word can turn. It can become something you didn't anticipate. My "year of joy" wasn't exactly that.

Instead it became a year where joy seemed to be just out of my reach. For every up, a down quickly followed. I kept losing sight of joy. It evaded my grasp. I wanted to be joy-filled, joy-full. And yet my circumstances kept making that nearly impossible.

In the course of that year I lost several things that were valuable to me — positions and people included. Plus, my family dealt with financial stress and setbacks. It seemed I could hardly rejoice in the "ups" before a "down" came along to blindside me.

About halfway through the year I began to grasp what exactly God had been up to when he let me choose JOY. Instead of making this a year filled with joy as I had naively assumed, he'd led me to select a word I'd need to work to take hold of. I'd have to literally choose joy when what I was apt to do was choose woe. Joy, I was learning, was a slippery little thing. And yet, because it was on my mind as my one word, I was determined to find it.

As I reflect back on my year with JOY, I see the benefits of having had that word as my focus. Had I not been seeking joy, I'd probably have missed it, getting mired in my circumstances instead of ferreting joy out of the nooks and crannies of my life. What I learned about joy is that, miraculously, you can find it. Even in unlikely places, even in the midst of some unsavory circumstances.

Don't assume that your word choice is going to be a passport to a life of ease. It may not be even if your one word is JOY. But realize that your word can bring you some lessons you wouldn't have learned any other way; lessons that will stay with you long after the year is over.

■ ■ ■

Marybeth is right. We can plan for a joyful year, but God may decide to use a year of difficulties to teach us that our source of strength is the joy of the Lord (Nehemiah 8:10). Which is better: God granting you twelve cushy months of ease, or learning how to find joy in the midst of struggles? Of course I'd say the former if we didn't both know that life is not a long succession of cushy years.

At times our word will seem to morph like this. We thought it was about one thing when we chose it, but it turns out God has something more or different in mind. I count this as one of the best parts of the My One Word exercise. This is how the project of choosing a single word and focusing on it for a year starts having unexpected and far-reaching effects.

### *Yield to Him*

Choosing a word like JOY doesn't buy you a blissful year to come. Being led by God to choose the word JOY doesn't ensure it either; Marybeth showed us that.

Neither does choosing a word like SACRIFICE or BROKENNESS guarantee you an incredibly difficult year. It could be a year of demanding circumstances, or it could be a year that you learn to stay broken before the Lord in the face of great success. Or perhaps it will become a year you sacrifice on behalf of others who are broken. You simply want to see what God is doing and where he is leading.

We make our plans, but ultimately the Lord directs our steps. That truth is laid out in Proverbs 16:9. Your one word will help you remain submissive.

Making plans is prudent. Preparation is critical, and vision is vital. But all of our carefully crafted strategies and well-meaning intentions must be surrendered to God's purposes. We allow him to direct our steps. And our word will morph in the direction he leads.

I suggested that you allow some time for your one word to arise when choosing it. Now let me add, don't shy away from "difficult" words. Our greatest growth often happens in the face of challenges, not in the absence of them.

When I pick a word that challenges me — maybe it reminds me of my incompetency in some area — it simultaneously keeps me humble and hopeful for change in Christ. That's a great position to stay in!

Once it's chosen, allow your word to morph. Allow God to transform it into something you didn't expect. Let it take on shades of meaning you didn't readily see. Permit it to become about something you didn't anticipate. Let it move beyond the initial reason for which you chose it.

Let God establish your steps as he leads you with your one word.

### *Unexpected Lessons*

A couple of years ago my wife turned forty. In my opinion she's as young, vibrant, and beautiful as the day I married her nearly twenty years ago. Besides, forty was not much different in my mind than thirty-eight or thirty-six.

Forty may be the new thirty, but this new decade does mark a major milestone. It is the midlife welcome sign. Forty is the excuse for convertibles and skydiving.

Turning forty not only influenced Julie's word choice that year, but it became her word for that year. Soon after choosing FORTY, however, her word began to morph. I'll let her tell you about it:

### Julie Ashcraft and FORTY

FORTY was my one word a couple of years ago. I mean I'm married to Mr. My One Word, and he always had the best words, so I was trying to come up with something creative and life changing. This would be the year that I turned forty, so I totally knew FORTY was going to be my word.

I can still remember when I was in elementary school and forty seemed so old. Now, however, forty was going to be the new thirty, or even twenty as far as I was concerned. I picked that word with the idea that I was going to institute a lot of "forties" in my life that would result in some real life change. Above all else, I wanted to lose weight and get in shape so I could feel better about myself. And by getting healthy, I would be a better Christian.

So I set out to do some "forty things." Here are just a few I had planned for that year:

- Lose forty pounds
- Spend forty minutes doing my quiet time each day
- Exercise forty minutes a day
- Drink forty ounces of water a day

I think you get the drift.

So off I started in the FORTY direction. Things were going great until I realized a month or two in why was I doing some of these "forty" things. It was driven out of fear that I was not good enough. And that Christ would not help me with them. That he might not meet me right where I was when I was scared or when I felt like I wasn't good enough. I glanced at my word and noticed that inside the word FORTY is the word FORT.... I knew right then that my word was changing into FORT-y. In all my times of fear, whether it was feelings of depression or not being good enough, I knew that Christ was calling me to run to him, and he would be my fortress.

Psalm 62:2 says, "Truly he is my rock and my salvation; he is my fortress, I will never be shaken." He would be the foundation upon which I would live out FORT-y.

I looked up in a concordance all the times the word *fort* or *fortress* was mentioned in the Bible. I printed those verses on one sheet and kept them. Each time that I felt like I needed to do these things for my self-worth, I would dive into Scripture and call to mind that Christ is my fortress, and he alone supplies my self-worth.

My whole perspective changed. I still used FORTY as my guideline to institute some good principles in my life that year, but my heart was changed in a way that I never dreamed about when I first chose the word.

So FORTY — or rather FORT-y! That was my one word.

## STEP

At first I chose STEP because of something Mike said about learning to walk with God. It occurred to me that I am trying to run with God rather than walk, and that I need to take it one step at a time. And that I need to be okay when I trip and fall. But since choosing it, I also feel it will help me with stepping out of my comfort zone and stepping out of my old ways and habits to become the person God wants me to be.

*—Jen*

## *Don't Abandon It*

As you spend time with God and with your word, you will see how it morphs to keep you moving in the direction God intends. You may make plans, but he directs your steps.

Pray and ask God to use your word to show you what you are missing, what you're not yet seeing. Check your motives for choosing your word and ask God what his motives are for you walking an entire year with this one word.

There may come a point in the year when you feel you've reached a standstill with your word. You've researched it, thought about it, prayed over it, looked for it to turn up in your life, sought to apply it, and then it seems to run dry. Nothing new is rising to the surface.

You may be tempted to abandon the project or pick a new word. Don't quit!

Don't give up; let it morph.

Begin to think creatively about your word. Let it spread and branch out. Think in new directions. Pray and ask God to expand your vision for your word. Consider what else it could apply to. Return to the Scriptures and read more about your word or the concept it encapsulates. And ask God to convict you where you need it but haven't yet realized it.

Change is possible, but focus is required. Remain focused on your one word and open to discover what you may have overlooked. Consider what God could have in mind for you this year with this word.

God's ways are higher than our ways. You can be sure that the reasons he is changing you are higher as well. So let your vision morph along with your character.

The verb *morph* means "to transform." And that's precisely what God does with our perspective and our character when we allow our one word to morph, when we allow him to direct and accomplish his purposes. And Julie showed us that.

### PATIENCE

Well, I did it! I picked PATIENCE. Any time I told someone that I was planning on picking PATIENCE, they would say, "Oh no. Be careful what you ask for there!" I was nervous but I took the jump. In my mind I thought that I was picking PATIENCE because I knew my husband and I would be trying to get pregnant this year, and my patience would wither away each month that passed and I was not pregnant. Only I got pregnant right away! And I soon realized what I was going to need patience for: the pregnancy. I am a control freak and when I start forgetting things, feeling sick when I had other plans, and hardly being able to keep my eyes open during a meeting, I lose patience with myself. I am learning to take one day at a time and to be PATIENT and wait on God and his process, not mine.

—*Melissa*

## *Flip It*

God moves in mysterious ways, including through our willingness to focus on a single word. First, he may move in us to choose a particular word when we go through the careful, prayerful process of selection. When that happens, we feel certain he led us to our word. We may also feel certain we know why.

But we may be off or shortsighted in our assumptions.

God will work through our word to bring about his purposes and our maturity, regardless of how we thought the year would go, regardless of our plans for our word, and regardless of our reasons for choosing it. So there may come a point when we sense our word is morphing.

Numerous My One Word followers report choosing a word

that would address a bothersome flaw or a particular desire they have, only to see that word "flip" and encompass more of God's purposes for them. They always consider this morph evidence of God leading them, communicating with them, and maturing them through their word.

Don't abandon your word if things aren't going as you planned. Let it morph. It is fine to make plans, but always stay submissive to God's moves to establish your steps as you walk through this year with your word.

Morphing is one way that this project of choosing a single word and focusing on it for an entire year has unexpected and far-reaching results. Another is that our word becomes the lens through which we examine *all* aspects of our lives. I'll talk about that in the next chapter, along with telling an embarrassing family story about my brother. I can't wait!

## *Reflect*

- Begin to think creatively about your word. Let it spread out and branch out. Think in new directions.
- Pray and ask God to expand your vision for your word. Record his response.
- Consider what else your one word could encompass.
- Return to Scripture and read more about your one word or the concept it encapsulates. Memorize additional verses about your word.

Chapter 8

# SEEING THROUGH YOUR WORD

*Now faith is confidence in what we hope for and assurance about what we do not see.*

— Hebrews 11:1

"Your brother just cleared the beach. Hilarious!"

This was the text message from my wife as I sat in a staff meeting while my vacationing family enjoyed a beautiful day at Wrightsville Beach. I couldn't wait to hear this.

I am the middle son. I have a brother to the north and one to the south. You can imagine the competitive chaos we generated around our house for most of our growing-up years.

My older brother, Mark, is the athlete and the one who can fix anything. My younger brother, Brian, is personable and the guy who can get anybody to do anything — a characteristic that would be a great benefit for his role as the beach-clearer. And I ... Well, I am the favorite son (I have a T-shirt to prove it!), but that has nothing to do with the story.

Brian spent the past decade in the snow-covered mountains

of Utah, which is light-years from the ocean. And as with most people who live landlocked, a trip to the beach inevitably spurs suspicions about sharks.

As a surfer, I spend a great deal of time in the ocean. Only once have I gotten out of the water because I felt threatened by a shark, even though the sharks are out there all the time. But because of Discovery Channel's "Shark Week," the movie *Jaws*, and our love of drama, people always talk about sharks at the beach.

Scary makes a good story, and people fear sharks. It doesn't matter that most people have never actually seen a shark outside of an aquarium.

Once a year the entire Ashcraft family comes to North Carolina to spend a week near me at Wrightsville Beach. My parents, grandparents, two brothers and their families — we all enjoy the beach and make memories together. And I usually give a surf lesson or two. It's become a tradition.

This sunny Tuesday morning the beach was moderately crowded, mostly locals at the place where our families were spending the day. Mostly locals, except for my brother from Utah.

The six Ashcraft cousins are splashing in the surf just offshore. The adults relax in beach chairs a short distance away. The day is gorgeous, and the blue-green water, calm. But it's all about to be interrupted by my younger sibling, who is on lifeguard duty watching the kids.

As he's scanning the ocean like a salty seaman, he sees a fin break the surface. He rubs his land-loving eyes to be sure of what he has seen. He needs to be certain before he swings into action.

Sure enough, he sees the fin again. It is time for some lifesaving heroics.

His voice breaks the serenity of the summer scene. Remember, this is the guy who can get anybody to do anything.

"SHHHHAAAARRRRRKKKKK!!!!" His voice echoes across the beach. "Everybody out of the water!"

Brian runs into the surf and helps the little kids to the safety of the sand. Then he sounds the alarm again to all in the vicinity to ensure the welfare of every beachgoer: "SHHAARRKK! Out of the water!"

Standing on the shore, the scared kids stare at the water looking for signs of the averted danger. Other people are looking too. Thanks to my brother, the hero, everyone has managed to get out of harm's way. His heart is racing and his adrenaline pumping, but he's relieved that the water is now devoid of people.

Standing there among the crowd of perceived admirers, Brian takes a moment to bask in the glory of his deed well done. He confesses to one of the onlookers, "Whew! I have never seen a shark in person before!"

To which a local gentleman responds, "Sir, you still haven't. Those are dolphins."

We had a great time retelling that tale all week. And we've since made Brian the official shark patrol of the annual Ashcraft family vacation.

Ever notice how easy it is to see what we expect to see?

## *We See What We Look For*

Human observations are biased toward confirming the observer's conscious and unconscious expectations. Psychologists call this tendency "the confirmation bias." This just means that our expectations, preconceptions, and core beliefs typically influence our interpretation of new information. Over and over experiments have proved that we see what we expect to see and conclude what we expect to be true.

To my land-loving lifeguard of a brother, every fin looks like a shark. He sees what he *fears* he'll see. It's sad how often what we fear frames what we see.

And what we refuse to see.

## INSPIRED

I do tons of dreaming about finished projects. Meanwhile the left-undone lies all around my life like yard-sale debris. I am putting the INSPIRED goggles on and am bringing completeness to my world of incompleteness.

*—Jim*

A few years ago, I built an addition onto my house. I constructed a fourteen-by-twenty-foot room off the back of my home with a loft overlooking the space below — complete with a spiral staircase leading to the loft. I was tremendously proud of this accomplishment.

A few months and a few storms later, I thought I saw a small bump on the wooden laminate flooring near the French doors. It looked like warping, but I decided I couldn't be sure. Maybe the angle was funny or shadows were playing tricks on my eyes. It was probably nothing.

After more weeks and more rain, my wife asked if I noticed anything wrong with the floor. She saw a problem.

"I don't see anything." I shrugged. I turned a blind eye.

Should I have been more diligent and checked it out carefully? Yes. But I didn't really want to know the truth. I didn't want to see anything wrong, because I didn't want to have to deal with anything wrong.

Then one winter day, the sun was low in the sky and shining through the French door windows just right. In that light, I saw. The buckled floor was unmistakable. Something was wrong and something clearly had to be done.

I had mistakenly behaved as if not noticing the problem would mean I'd never have to address it. How often do we do *that*? In reality, I'd only delayed the inevitable while the problem got bigger. It's all too easy to let our fears control what we see.

Our fears unconsciously frame what we see and what we don't. Failing to see or refusing to see always costs us. That's because what we see determines the direction we will go.

## *Sight Determines Direction*

The attention of our eyes focuses the affection of our hearts. Advertisers lure our hearts with images that appeal to our eyes. They know that what we see determines the direction we will go. Set your eyes on that new purchase, and your life will move in the direction of the fulfillment of that vision.

The eyes in our head show us a reality based on what we can see and touch. The eyes of our heart, once enlightened — to borrow a phrase from Paul — show us a reality that our physical eyes cannot see. A reality based on the words and promises of God.

God promises his presence. God promises his faithfulness. He promises his goodness, his provision, and his power. He promises all of that is there for us, in spite of what we face.

God promises that he is always working in our lives, and he ensures that everything works together to serve his purposes (Romans 8:28). Even when our eyes can't see it being worked out.

Noah trusted God and built an ark before his eyes spotted the first dark clouds. Abraham trusted God and journeyed to a land he'd never seen. Moses rejected the shiny treasures of Pharaoh to receive the riches of Christ, whom he'd never laid eyes on.

Hebrews 11 continues the list of people who trusted God's promises when they could not see them. This chapter of the Bible begins by saying, "Now faith is being sure of what we hope for and certain of what we do not see" (Hebrews 11:1).

Our hope for change and spiritual formation requires faith. Are you certain God will change you with regards to your one word this year? We need faith in order to see what our eyes can't. We need eyes of faith to follow God. Paul writes in 2 Corinthians 5:7, "We walk by faith, not by sight" (ESV).

Faith is the way in which we perceive the reality in which we live. We either walk by faith, trusting in the promises and the reality of God. Or we walk by sight, believing only in what we've seen or trusting only what we can touch.

We're told to fix our eyes on Christ and walk by faith, because what we see will determine what we believe and the direction we will go.

---

**RUN**

---

RUN is a relevant word to me because I ran year-round from sixth grade until my freshman year in college. Running is not passive. It requires focus, conscientious action, determination, strength, and a desire to reach a tangible destination. This year I hope to use RUN as a lens in a few key aspects. First, I desire to run from temptation, just as Joseph ran from Potiphar's wife. Second, I want to run to Jesus, the answer to all my needs. Third, I want to run to be healthier so I might better serve God. In using RUN as a lens, I hope to see my moral, spiritual, and physical self grow stronger this year.

*—Elliot*

### *Framing What We See*

There is a way to consciously frame our vision. I realized this one evening while watching our local government TV channel. I know what you're thinking: who watches that channel? Apparently me, though not habitually, I assure you.

Nevertheless, I was watching the TV as our local building-code official gave some kind of safety talk to a group of officials listening with forced interest. (And here I was tuned in voluntarily.) What caught my attention was the passion with which the woman spoke about something I rarely give thought to: building safety.

As a former architecture student, I could appreciate the topic to a degree. She spoke with a sense of urgency. "We need a more pronounced focus on safety signage, equipment, and procedures," she warned. By the time she got to the section of her speech on emergency egress, I was glued. She spoke as though our lives depended upon it. And lives do.

Her passion grew with the length of her speech. The climax of her talk turned personal as she said that she could not go anywhere without looking for exit signs and fire extinguishers. Everywhere she went — restaurants, theaters, shopping malls — whether on duty or off, she noticed each building's safety features.

That's because she's trained her eyes to see those. She sees what she has *taught* herself to see. For her, building safety has become a lens through which she sees every building.

Each year, that's my goal for my one word. I want to train my eyes to look at my world — all of it — through the lens of my one word. I need to learn to *see* differently, if I am going to *live* differently.

### *Seeing and Living Differently*

Did you have a specific area of your life and not just a certain aspect of your character in mind when you chose your one word? I did when I chose the word FINISH in 2007.

I selected the word FINISH because I found myself allowing things at work to remain in a state of "almost complete" or a state of "good enough" instead of following through and finishing them. Various initiatives and projects sat half started. And lots of books sat half read.

*What is wrong with me that I have so many unfinished tasks?*

*Why can't I complete the things I want to do?*

*Why do I make excuses for things left undone?*

*Why do I take shortcuts and deliver less than my best?*

*Why do I start new things before I've completed the current project?*

*Why can't I even finish the books I begin?*

I wanted to be the kind of person who would diligently see things through, so I picked FINISH. I hoped it would give me the tenacity on the job that I felt I needed to keep my edge. So my one word began with a focus on work tasks and study habits. But it became about so much more.

By three months into it I'd gotten pretty tenacious about completing tasks at work. I was paying much more attention to my follow-through and choosing new projects carefully. I avoided saying yes to more things than I could realistically complete. With each opportunity that presented itself, I'd ask, "If I start this, can I finish it? What will I have to leave undone to complete this?" I was prioritizing and structuring my day differently with the word FINISH.

I'd also developed some habits to help me finish each day at my office. First, I'd tie up any loose ends that could be quickly addressed. Then, I'd unclutter my desk. And finally, I'd make a to-do pile for the next day of anything not-yet finished (also known as the procrastination pile; My One Word isn't about perfection but the process of change).

It was working. FINISH was helping me in the ways I'd envisioned it would. I was reading entire books and completing projects that I could've let slide without anyone noticing. And I could see God working on my character. I was becoming a finisher.

I'd selected a passage from James 1:4, which reads, "Let perseverance finish its work so that you may be mature and complete, not lacking anything." When I struggled to complete a task or see a matter through, I used this verse to remind me endurance is necessary to finish God's work of maturing me. It enabled me to see my struggles as a critical part of my growth.

### *From a Goal to a Lens*

One evening after a busy but productive day at work, I left my tidied desk and procrastination pile and headed home. Everything in me wanted the to-dos of my life to be over at five o'clock that day. But there was soccer practice, dinner, and cleanup. Once dinner was finished, there was still kids' homework, bath time, and school lunches to pack.

*Just plow through*, I thought. *The end is near*. I envisioned climbing into the recliner and doing nothing more than staring at *Sports Center*. And this is where my one word took a real turn for me.

The end of my day *was* near, but it hadn't yet ended.

It dawned on me that I was resolving to simply endure, to trudge through the rest of my day, and this startled me. Sounds more dramatic than it was, but here's the point: That's not what a finisher would do. That's not how a finisher views his or her life.

Suddenly I was looking at what I was thinking and doing while off work through the lens of my one word. Finishing the rest of the day didn't make my radar until I turned around and saw soccer practice, dinner, homework, bath, and bedtime as multiple opportunities to finish well.

If someone were to ask me that morning to describe a good finish to my day, I would never talk about rushing through dinner, begrudgingly packing lunches, pushing through bath time, and then putting the kids to bed with minimum effort and connection all so I could drop myself in front of the TV and mindlessly watch guys play with bats or clubs.

So a quarter of the way through my year with FINISH I applied it to my home life too. My word allowed me to see that my day had a conclusion beyond the end of the work day.

At that point FINISH moved from a goal to a lens for me.

From there I taught myself to look at my life through the lens of my one word. It became the filter through which I viewed every aspect: my work life, home life, weekends, relationships, social obligations, everything. That's how this word paid big dividends well beyond a tidy desk and stack of read books.

Had I not peered through the lens of this word, my days would have come to one rolling stop after another, time endured rather than time redeemed. My one word managed to redeem my view of, and attitude toward, all my daily obligations. Not just those prior to my evening commute home.

We drift into the patterns of our lives unintentionally, because we don't have anything else training our view. Your one word can frame your view this year. Train yourself to look through it.

Let me show how that might work. Imagine you chose the word LIGHTEN because you wanted to lose some weight this year. Terrific. But as your year progresses, consider applying your word to aspects of your life beyond your weight.

What about your mind? Do you need to lighten your stress? To cast your cares on Christ and worry less?

Do you need to lighten your home? Could it use a serious decluttering? Is it time to downsize?

Is there regular conflict in your marriage or in your workplace? What can you do to lighten the tone?

What about your finances? Is there a debt that is weighing you down? What can you do to lighten your debt load this year?

When you begin seeing your world through the lens of your one word, opportunities for action and growth abound. Don't get overwhelmed by the opportunities; you don't have to take them all. Remember, you just have to do something about one thing this year. This isn't about perfection but progress.

But as you get a handle on one aspect of your one word, keep looking. Keep seeing your life through the lens of your one word. God is doing, and plans to do, far more than your eyes can now see.

---

### CONSISTENT

I grew up in the church and had always been involved until my brother died when I was seventeen. This sent me in a spiral going nowhere. I got deeply involved with drugs and music—and I mean deep—until ten years later (about nine months ago) when I got arrested for possession of heroin. I took a look at my life and was just like, *Wow. Where did the past ten years go? How did I get here?* So two days later I attended this church, because in my heart I knew what was right. It changed my life. I now attend a weekly small group (which, crazy story, happens to be in the exact same apartment I used to get my drugs from not even a year ago, till my dealer got arrested and my leader moved in!). I also started serving at the church. Everything has been absolutely amazing ever since. The problem is I am not CONSISTENT in my faith, in my prayers, in my thoughts, or in my all-around love for people. I am really excited about this project and can't wait to share how it is changing my life.

—*Joe*

## *Seeing Life through the Lens*

If you don't keep your word in front of you, you'll likely forget your word. If you don't forget it, you'll be tempted at some point to quit your word. If you don't quit your word, it will change the way you see. And when it changes the way you see, it will change the way you live.

We can look at ourselves through the lens of our one word and see room for growth. But the potential of a word to act as a lens is not simply to put ourselves under a microscope and find every flaw.

We can look at God through the lens of our one word and see where our grace and help comes from.

We can look at others, too, through the lens of our one word. Realizing that our gifts and talents, entrusted to us by God, are needed in this world. That's what my current one word INVEST is doing for me.

And we can look at the events of our lives through the lens of our one word and discover that each of them comes to us sifted through the hands of a trustworthy God.

My One Word provides us with a lens, with a new way of seeing. It's a tool to train our eyes. It helps us frame the way we process the world around us and what happens to us. And it keeps us hoping and believing that God is always forming us and changing us, and there is no circumstance that can prevent that.

Early one Saturday morning, my family and I had just finished breakfast when my phone buzzed. My assistant was calling to advise me to check my email. Something had happened.

I grabbed my second cup of coffee and my laptop and headed for the quiet of my bedroom. Before reading the email I noted it had been sent at 1:32 a.m. While I was sleeping soundly, the fingers of a burdened mother had been typing the account of the circumstances that left her heart heavy.

She'd just become a grandmother; her grandson had been born a month premature. There had been some complications with his lungs, but that's not why she was writing.

I read the email slowly, going over every word.

*Dear Mike,*

*My husband and I are members of the church. It is with a very heavy heart and a broken spirit that I wish to inform you of our twenty-year-old daughter's death on Friday, December 18, 2009. What started out as a very joyous occasion soon turned for the worst.*

*Our daughter was in the hospital expecting her first child. It was a premature delivery at thirty-three weeks and four days. She gave birth to a beautiful baby boy and his name is Benjamin. The baby is in neonatal care at New Hanover Regional Hospital and is doing well at this point.*

*Unfortunately, our daughter put all of her life and energy into bringing him into this world and had an amniotic embolism. And did not survive.*

*I wish to ask you to pray for the family as she has several sisters. I thank God for the time we did have with our precious daughter, and I know we do not always understand God's ways, but I know he is always with us. And I trust him in this situation — my one word for this year has been TRUST.*

*I have gone through many situations this year, and I have learned to trust God. No matter how dark things look, I trust him because he always has our best interest at heart. My daughter, Kaitlin Parker, knew Jesus, and I can rest in the assurance that she is with the Lord.*

*Thank you for your prayers,*

*Robert and Christy Berg*

Christy's perspective in light of her loss is astonishing. And commendable. But what really strikes me is how quickly she got there. Her beloved daughter died, leaving a newborn motherless, and Christy sent me the email that very night before going to sleep. Not a month, a week, or even a full day had yet passed.

Of course Christy wasn't done processing the magnitude of the event. But look how quickly she was able to land in the healthy position of TRUST. That's because she'd spent a year training herself to look at every aspect of her life through her one word.

Christy saw what she expected to see, even when she faced the unexpected. We are always going to have a confirmation bias. The question is what will it confirm: our fears or our faith?

What will you see when you look through the lens of your one word?

Use your one word to begin training your perspective. Change is possible. Great change is possible, but focusing through the lens of your one word is required.

In the final chapter I'll tell you more about how I ended each day with FINISH as my lens, but before that I want to tell you how your word can be a powerful tool in the heat of the moment or in the midst of distraction. Turn to the next chapter and learn how to blow up those moments.

## *Reflect*

- Begin looking at different aspects of your day through the lens of your one word.
- Consider how your word might apply to your work life, your home life, your family life, your hobbies, your friendships, your dreams, your health, your finances, your reputation, your faith.
- What fears and desires have been driving what you see?
- How has what you've seen, or expected to see, determined the direction you have gone?
- How can your one word redirect you this year?

## Chapter 9

# BLOW UP THE MOMENT

*Do not be conformed to this world,*
*but be transformed by the renewal of your mind,*
*that by testing you may discern what is the will of God,*
*what is good and acceptable and perfect.*
— Romans 12:2 ESV

Henri Nouwen once said our inner life — the life of the mind — is like a banana tree full of jumping monkeys.[6] I love that.

His assessment brought me great relief. Until then I'd wondered if something was seriously wrong with me. Why couldn't I concentrate or pray for more than a few minutes at a time? Why was I so easily distracted from my goals? Why did I sometimes feel at odds with myself? Did I have ADD?

As it turns out most people have a mind full of monkeys.

Too many of us assume we can't do anything about the monkeys. So we tolerate them, play with them, and allow them to

6 Henri J. M. Nouwen, *The Way of the Heart: Connecting with God through Prayer, Wisdom, and Silence* (New York: Ballantine Books, 1981), 18.

roam undeterred — not realizing the guerilla warfare they wage on our souls.

---

### PURIFY

Lately, I noticed that my language and thought life were in contradiction with the life I claim to live and want to live. So I picked PURIFY in hopes that I can use this word to make changes in every aspect of my life.

*— Logan*

---

### *It's Not a Game*

She had no idea how badly I wanted to win.

She was about six and I was about twenty-six. We met at a backyard vacation Bible school in Surf City, North Carolina. The idea of backyard Bible club is to play games with the kids, have fun together, earn their respect, and teach them about Jesus.

The activity was called "Animal Relay," and the objective was clear: the first team to cross the finish line wins. The rules are simple. Two teams form two lines. The gun sounds and each line follows the basic formula of a relay race. One runner at a time races toward the cone several yards in front of them. They circle the cone and return to their line, tagging the next person.

The animal part of the relay is that we didn't simply run to the cone and back; we had to imitate a given animal as we went. Each team alternated choosing the required animal to imitate next.

"Chicken!"

The racers strut and cluck their way to the cone, flapping their elbows like wings.

"Frog!"

Hop and ribbit down and back.

"Horse!"

Rear up, neigh, and take off galloping.

I think you get the idea.

The race was close. It was coming down to the anchors in the final run on each team: me and Sarah. She was smiling and excited. I was focused and determined. Little Sarah had seriously underestimated who she was dealing with.

It was my turn to call out the animal. As my teammate tagged my hand, I shouted, "Raptor!"

Sarah had no idea what a raptor was. And no idea what was about to happen. I can do a mean velociraptor. *Jurassic Park* was at the peak of its popularity at the time, and I had the jump and the screech down.

I pulled my arms into my body and let them hang close with my hands tucked like claws. I pushed my head downward and outward projecting the fierce teeth of the dinosaur. My predator instincts were flowing. My legs, spring-loaded, were able to pounce on any prey that stood in my way. And with the race on the line, I sprang.

Leaping right up and over the top of Sarah's little head, I became the raptor. Like a scene from the movie, I whipped my head to the left and then back to the right and let out a loud, high-pitched sound.

"Screeeeecccch!"

Then I tore off toward the cone, leaving Sarah in the dust, terrified. She even cried.

I am not proud of this victory. My competitive mind monkeys were on the loose. That day they happened to want to be clever, to play raptor, and to beat the ponytailed little girl I'd come to teach about Jesus.

Little Sarah thought we were playing a friendly game. But I

was waging a war.[7] Ever notice how it only takes the intentions of one side to create war for both sides?

### *It's a War*

Satan's perpetual aim is to infiltrate our thoughts with his thoughts, promoting his lies over God's truth. If Satan can control our thoughts, he can control our behaviors.[8] This is a war — Satan has declared it — and your mind is ground zero.

If we fail to realize we're in a war, we'll fail to fight.

This is the problem most of us face when it comes to spiritual formation. We entertain racy, rude, or risqué thoughts, rather than taking them captive. We invite them in, point to the sofa, and say, "Make yourself at home. Can I get you a drink?" We cook them dinner. We converse with them, assuming we can ask them nicely to please leave at any time.

Thinking them harmless, we let the mind monkeys play a while, and eventually we join them. Sin begins as a thought, as a desire that is entertained. A thought that should have been captured but it appealed to our flesh in some way. And then it became a problem.

They might be cute — that's debatable I suppose — but most monkeys are far from harmless. I've watched a lot of Jeff Corwin on *Animal Planet*; monkeys are the only animal I've seen him visibly scared of, and I figure he knows what he's talking about.

We think we're playing harmless games when we let the monkeys run unchecked. In reality, they're leading us onto a battlefield. Our own flesh conspires against us in this battle, hijacking our thoughts with ungodly motives and desires.

---

7 While this story is true, Sarah was not scarred for life. We actually became great friends that week!

8 See David in 1 Chronicles 21:1, Judas in John 13:2, and Ananias in Acts 5:3.

Scripture describes a conflict raging between our flesh and our spirit. We are warned to pay close attention to the desires of our flesh because they "wage war against the soul" (1 Peter 2:11 NASB).

John Piper writes, "Until you believe that life is war — that the stakes are your soul — you will probably just play at Christianity with no bloodearnestness and no vigilance and no passion and no wartime mindset."[9]

I think it stands to reason, with no victory either.

We have to fight thoughts that would lead us astray. We have to counter them with truth. And we can't hesitate to be violent about it. Piper continues:

> There is a mean, violent streak in the true Christian life! But violence against whom or what? Not other people. It's a violence against all the impulses in us that would be violent to other people [including ponytailed little girls!]. It's a violence against all the impulses in our own selves that would make peace with our own sin and settle in with a peacetime mentality. It's a violence against all lust in ourselves, and enslaving desires for food or caffeine or sugar or chocolate or alcohol or pornography or money or the praise of men and the approval of others or power or fame.[10]

The life of the mind is lived on a battlefield full of banana trees. We can't just kick back and pretend it's a zoo. We can't just observe. We have to fight.

---

9 John Piper, "How to Kill Sin, Part 2," (February 17, 2002), http://www.desiringgod.org/resource-library/sermons/how-to-kill-sin-part-2
10 Ibid.

### *The Moment of Truth*

I will never forget the first time I realized the subtlety of this battle. It was late in the evening, and my daughter had trouble sleeping. So I brought her into the living room and laid her beside me on the couch. I rubbed her back while I watched *Sports Center* with the volume down low. She settled and eventually drifted into her dreams.

Feeling tired myself, I dreaded getting up to carry her to bed, so I decided to just chill out until the top ten plays were finished. Then I would carry her to her room before slipping into bed next to my wife.

I picked up the remote control to turn the TV off. In a flash — maybe out of habit, but not out of conscious intent — I flipped the channel. One click of the remote, then another, just to see what was on.

The mind monkeys were loose. Undetected, but loose.

Before I knew it, I was full-on channel surfing. Scanning the channels, looking for nothing in particular. Images of college students on spring break in Daytona arrested my attention. The monkeys began to jump.

There was a stage next to a pool filled with barely clad co-eds. The game they were about to play involved two of them, a guy and a girl, wrapping themselves in a large cloth, like some sort of human burrito. Shaving cream would play a major role in the game. I'm guessing beer did as well.

In less than a minute my mind had gone from getting ready for bed to a banana tree full of screaming monkeys. With my eyes on the TV, my mind moved in a thousand directions, banana peels dropping everywhere.

This would be the moment! You might say it was a moment of truth. But nevertheless it was only a moment.

I seized this point in time and examined what was going on in my head. The moment slowed down as I questioned the validity of my desires. *Why do I, a follower of Christ, want to stop and watch this? I'm happily married and am sitting here with my daughter. Why would I tolerate such thoughts? How can something that should disgust me look so appealing?*

I upped the intensity of the questions. *Would I want my own daughter wrapped up like a human burrito with an intoxicated college boy on that stage?* I looked down at the sweet girl sleeping serenely next to me. No! The idea sickened me.

The important part of this scenario is the fact that all of these questions had answers. But what was required was the space inside of a moment to examine my thoughts and actually make decisions according to what I knew to be true.

In that moment, the facts were not the issue; the truth was obvious. What had escaped me was how hard it can be to get to the truth when your senses are assaulted by deception. It always seems that the truth is seen in the 20/20 vision of hindsight.

---

## REPLACE

---

I struggle with constant negative thoughts in my day-to-day life having to do with self-confidence and confidence in being a mother and a wife. This year I want to focus on becoming someone who thinks positively, who thinks about all the blessings I have in my life. To focus on being thankful for these things and not letting the Devil steal my joy. I am choosing the word REPLACE and working to replace bad thoughts with Scripture and positive thinking. Philippians 4:8—to think on things that are pure, true, lovely, commendable, honorable. Things I want my daughters to see in me and my life. I want replacing bad thoughts with Scripture to become a lifelong habit or reflex, so I can become a person of confidence and contentment!

*—Casey*

It is critical to catch these thoughts before they lead you into temptation. James writes, "But each person is tempted when they are dragged away by their own evil desire and enticed. Then, after desire has conceived, it gives birth to sin" (James 1:14 – 15). Don't let your mind monkeys drag you away!

It can happen very innocently. But don't let it happen without notice.

On this night I saw the moment. I saw the *truth* in the moment. And I learned a new way to think about the battle in my mind.

I turned the TV off!

### *Taking Thoughts Captive*

That was the evening I realized I can think my own thoughts. I can actually choose what I will think about. I'm not at the whim of my mind monkeys. I'm not at the whim of my emotions. I'm not at the whim of the media. I'm not at the whim of my desires.

I'm also not at the whim of my enemy. I have been given the mind of Christ and I can think my thoughts (1 Corinthians 2:16).

Sure, thoughts will arise uninvited. Not all of them will be helpful, hopeful, or profitable. Some will be tempting. But I get to decide which ones I will entertain. I choose what I will dwell on.

---

**CHOOSE**

---

My one word is CHOOSE. Because in everything I can do or will do, I have a choice about how I respond. I hope this word will cause me to be accountable in how I react to things in my life and will help me take a moment to think before I act. To remember what is truly important instead of just responding with a quick worldly instinct or action.

*—Pam*

In fact, the Bible tells me to think intentionally. Philippians 4:8 says, "Finally, brothers and sisters, whatever is true, whatever is noble, whatever is right, whatever is pure, whatever is lovely, whatever is admirable — if anything is excellent or praiseworthy — think about such things." I am commanded to think. I am given a list of things to think about.

I can purposely bring such thoughts onto the scene to tranquilize the monkeys as long as I create the space in time to do it. I call this practice "blowing up the moment."

Think of Neo in the movie *The Matrix*. He found that in the split-second space between when a gun was fired at him and when the bullet reached him, he could use his mind to stop the bullet from entering his heart.

In my favorite scene, time seems to slow for just a second as Neo sees the bullets racing toward him. He raises his hand in a "stop" position. Using mental resistance, he slows the bullets to a stop, midair in front of him. Plucking one bullet out of the air and examining it, Neo then tosses it to the ground. The rest of the bullets fall as well, rendering his enemies powerless.

You and I can do this too, spiritually speaking.

Paul essentially instructs us to "blow up the moment" in 2 Corinthians 10:3 – 5: "For though we live as human beings, we do not wage war according to human standards, for the weapons of our warfare are not human weapons, but are made powerful by God for tearing down strongholds. We tear down arguments and every arrogant obstacle that is raised up against the knowledge of God, and we take every thought captive to make it obey Christ" (NET).

We can take our thoughts captive — every single one. How? First you must blow up the moment. Your reaction or mindless drift into temptation happens in a moment. You must create the space in that moment to see what is happening and then to make a decision. The key is to isolate and examine the specific thought or belief that's driving your desire in that moment. Take it captive; identify it. Then stack it up against the knowledge of God.

Against knowledge of Scripture.

Against your one word.

If the thought is not true, noble, right, pure, lovely, admirable, excellent, or praiseworthy, then get rid of it. It is to be destroyed. The Bible says, "*We are* destroying speculations and every lofty thing raised up against the knowledge of God" (2 Corinthians 10:5 NASB).

When we bring Scripture on the scene, we bring truth on the scene. At a minimum you will have memorized one verse about your word as part of the My One Word exercise. Remember those verses you looked up when choosing your word? Bring that verse on the scene. Call it to your mind. Your mind is where the process of spiritual formation is centered. That's why the battle in your mind is so critical to the condition of your heart.

The Bible teaches us that our mind must be dealt with in order for the heart to be transformed. Renewal in the head is essential to renewal in the heart. Read this familiar passage in Paul's letter to the Romans: "Therefore, I urge you, brothers and sisters, in view of God's mercy, to offer your bodies as a living sacrifice, holy and pleasing to God — this is your true and proper worship. Do not conform to the pattern of this world, but be transformed by the renewing of your mind. Then you will be able to test and approve what God's will is — his good, pleasing and perfect will" (Romans 12:1 – 2).

Discernment requires you to test what is happening in your head. Test your thoughts; they drive your actions and reactions. Test them against what God says is good. Test them against what you know about him and about his ways. Discern the truth and choose accordingly.

The prophet Jeremiah, writing some five hundred years before Paul, was teaching us about capturing thoughts and blowing up moments. You see an example of this recorded for us in the book of Lamentations: "I have been deprived of peace; I have forgotten what prosperity is. So I say, 'My splendor is gone and all that I had hoped from the LORD.' I remember my affliction and my wandering, the bitterness and the gall. I well remember them, and my soul is downcast within me. Yet this I call to mind and therefore I have hope: Because of the LORD's great love we are not consumed, for his compassions never fail. They are new every morning; great is your faithfulness. I say to myself, 'The LORD is my portion; therefore I will wait for him'" (Lamentations 3:17 – 24).

Jeremiah is pouring out his thoughts: *I've been deprived. I've had bitter hard times. My splendor is gone. God is not doing anything for me anymore.*

He is also noticing how these thoughts are making him feel: *I'm depressed. I feel defeated. My soul is downcast within me.*

Most of us don't have to work very hard to think negative thoughts. They just pop up. We have no problem thinking about the things we regret. We have no problem thinking about the problems and issues that overwhelm us. When our minds get set on these things, our hearts follow. When our minds are overwhelmed, our hearts feel the pressure.

But when we set our minds on the things of God and his truth, well, our hearts will follow in that direction as well. The key is that you have to actually put your mind to work to recall what is true. We see this as Jeremiah actively thinks his thoughts.

And this is the pivot point. The prophet says, "Yet this I call to mind ..." Then he lists what he knows to be true about God: *God's love keeps me from being consumed. God faithfully gives me fresh mercy and compassion each day. God is good to the one who seeks him.*

What's the result of Jeremiah blowing up this moment, of taking his thoughts captive and stacking them up against the knowledge of God? He tells us in verse 21, "I have hope." Taking his thoughts captive the prophet moves from "Woe is me, I'm depressed," to "God is wow, and I am blessed!" Hope wells up in his heart.

So pause, blow up the moment, and look at your thoughts. Examine and test them. Replace them, when necessary, with his truth. Replace them with your one word and the vision of the person you are becoming in Christ. This is how we fight.

### STEWARD

I was hit hard recently with the idea of mindset. Whatever you choose to set your thoughts on will find its way into your life. So I thought of the one word *money*. Hey, I like money! Then I thought *rich*, but both those speak to my selfish desires, not to a mind set on God. With either of those as My One Word, my mind would be focused entirely on acquiring money, and I wouldn't focus on God. After a lot of thought, I realized that my mindset and my one word needed to be STEWARD. I want to learn to disregard getting money and make my focus truly appreciating and valuing whatever it is that God gives me in life. If it's money, great. If not, I know God will provide. My mindset is to see and STEWARD my gifts this year.

—*Jason*

## *Making Mind Monkeys Mind*

My congregation will tell you I frequently advocate journaling as a spiritual practice. In fact, the next chapter is designed to help you begin this important exercise with your one word.

I practice what I preach too. I have to. For me, the renewal of my mind often involves writing things down. I monkey-wrangle best with a pen in my hand.

As I read my Bible each morning, I write. I write verses that stand out to me. I note what challenges me. I record questions I have for God. I write out prayers and answers to prayers. I write about my one word for the year. I examine my heart and confess in print what I'm struggling with. (Sometimes I resort to using code.)

One Sunday I told the crowd at Port City Community Church about the mind monkeys. I added, "I write stuff down to make the monkeys go where they're supposed to be." Later that week someone from the service tweeted: "Out of sync with myself today — thought, 'Write this crud down! Tell the monkeys where to go!' "

A somewhat crass description perhaps, but at least they now know how to do battle and re-sync. I didn't get any further tweets; I assume writing down her out-of-sync thoughts helped her blow up the moment too. Sir Francis Bacon wrote, "Reading maketh a full man ... writing an exact man." The mind monkeys need to be told exactly what to do. We cannot risk being unclear when so much is at stake.

For me, putting thoughts to paper is a surefire way of taking them captive. So is quoting Scripture. Psalm 119:11 tells us plainly to hide God's Word in our heart so that we will be less likely to sin against him. Capture your thoughts in your mind and hide God's Word in your heart and you've got a powerhouse weapon in the battle of the mind.

So next time you find yourself face-to-face with a mind monkey, blow up the moment. Don't blow the moment; blow it up. Pause and gain perspective. Bring your one word to bear on your situation. You have a choice about what you will think and how you will respond.

If you can get to paper and pen, write it down. What are you actually thinking? Why are you thinking it? What should you think instead? Search Scripture for truth to counteract the monkey screams. Remember, we don't fight with mere human willpower but with Spirit-fueled truth. And sometimes with a pen.

In the next chapter, I'll go into detail on using a pen and paper to take thoughts captive and track your progress this year with your one word. Don't miss that.

The path of transformation is marked by the renewing of our minds. Capturing our thoughts prepares us to live from new hearts. Listen to Paul, imitate Jeremiah, and blow up the moments.

Wield your one word alongside the sword of the Spirit. Make the monkeys go where they belong, and make them take their banana peels with them.

The monkeys might be inevitable but they are not undefeatable.

### *Reflect*

- Think about your one word and the common stumbling blocks you encounter. Then compile a list of Scriptures that will help you blow up the moment.
- Begin memorizing the verses on your list.
- Pay attention to your banana tree this week. When necessary, write to make the monkeys go where they need to be.

## Chapter 10

# WRITE YOUR GUTS OUT

*I was in the Spirit on the Lord's day,*
*and I heard behind me a loud voice*
*like the sound of a trumpet, saying,*
*"Write in a book what you see ..."*
— REVELATION 1:10 – 11 NASB

It was a beautiful Friday afternoon in November. The air temperature reached 64 degrees and the water temp matched. It was a perfect day to sneak in a lunchtime surf session. So I took off from the office and headed to my house to load my surfboard on my car, slip into my wetsuit, and seize the opportunity.

I make it a habit to call my wife and let her know that I will be away from my phone while I am surfing, so she won't wonder why she can't catch up with me should she call. This day she didn't answer, so I left a message: "Hey, babe! I'm stopping for gas and am going to catch a couple of waves for lunch. Love you!"

There are two things you need to know. First, the low fuel light was on in my wife's van that morning; her vehicle needed gas too. And second, she has an app on her phone that transcribes her voicemails and then texts them to her.

So while I was headed to the beach that morning, my sweet wife was sitting in a meeting with her coworkers. Her phone vibrated, indicating she has missed a call (from me).

A few seconds later it vibrated again, indicating she has received a text message (the transcript of my call). The text message transcription of my voicemail read: “Hey, babe! I am coming to get you gas and bring you by some lunch. Love you!”

You can imagine her delight at the idea of her thoughtful husband driving all the way across town to fill up her van because he knows how much she hates getting gas. And he’s bringing her lunch as well. She’s so touched, she reads it out loud to everyone in the meeting. There’s a collective *awww.*

Her coworkers headed off to Subway without her while she waited for me. Only I never arrived.

Words are critical to our perspective; they must be accurate to aid our understanding. Transcription apps are cool things, but ultimately Julie needed to hear my own words that day to understand what was truly going on with me.

Day in and day out, I need to hear my own words to understand what’s going on with me too.

In this chapter, I am going to share with you the most powerful tool I’ve found for walking through a year with my one word. In the coming pages, I want to urge you, encourage you, inspire and challenge you to get your own words down on paper this year by keeping a journal. This will help you understand what is truly going on with you, with you and God, and with your one word.

## *Getting to the Guts*

In his memoir, pastor Eugene Peterson explains the benefit of putting written words to our experiences, particularly our experiences with God. He insists that writing helps him pay attention, learn, and pray. And writing helps him discover what he didn't realize before he put pen to paper.

That's an interesting thing about language. When you give words to something, you not only label it; you discover its essence and define its meaning as well. It's not just a recording of what you know but a discovery of what you didn't yet see.

Peterson says that writing helps him "get to the guts" of who he is.[11] He describes journaling as "a way of entering into language and letting language enter me, words connecting with words creating what had previously been inarticulate or unnoticed or hidden."[12]

We, too, need to notice what might be hidden or hiding. We need to see what is truly going on with us. Writing helps both Peterson and me to see ourselves. I see the guts of who I am, and who I am in Christ. The words in my journals connect the dots for me of how Christ's character is being displayed in my life and formed in my heart.

## TRUST

My word is TRUST. I have subtle fears that were almost impossible to see until God pulled back the veil and showed me. They're small fears that I've ignored or not recognized before, but now I can see the areas where I lacked trust in the Lord. This revelation rocked me completely, but it is so amazing to see the Lord working! I am giving him these areas bit by bit, and his Holy Spirit is speaking to me and leading me. I took Mike's advice and have started journaling. What an awesome thing!

—*Emily*

11 Eugene H. Peterson, *The Pastor: A Memoir* (New York: HarperOne, 2011), 238.
12 Ibid., 239.

## *It's All Good*

I am not really a food guy. All my life I've stuck to meat, potatoes, and pizza. Plus, I'm a food separatist; I don't like the different foods on my plate to touch. Basically, my palate hasn't progressed much since middle school.

I am not a foodie but I do like to eat. And though I don't have a refined sense of taste, I am warming to the idea of learning to appreciate food more. Perhaps I am on the cusp of a culinary transformation?

If so, no doubt part of this transformation can be traced to my favorite show on the Food Network, *Chopped*. It showcases four chefs in a competition for a cash prize.

A panel of food-loving judges critiques the chefs' creations, and round by round, the chef of the least-liked food is "chopped" from the competition until only two remain. They compete in the dessert round where the winner walks away with ten grand.

The best part is that every round contains a mystery basket of ingredients that must be included in each chef's dish. The basket holds crazy items like blue-toed chicken, gooey duck, black licorice, bok choy, or yucca plant.

I'm absolutely fascinated watching these chefs creatively combine the ingredients. In thirty minutes they make something that actually looks appetizing to me, a staunch burger-and-fries guy. Their understanding of how flavors work boggles my mind. I wouldn't know where to begin.

But the judges were what caught my attention when I first began watching. They take a bite of each dish, contemplate it, and then describe what they experienced in great detail. They talk about layers of flavors and textures. I'd never heard such descriptions of how a food tasted.

Assertive, timid, delicate, calming, vibrant, earthy, velvety.

They make statements like, "The flavor profile you achieved here — bright citrus enhancing the smoky-sweet depth — provides an unexpected assertiveness to this dish." Aware of their own taste buds, they find nuanced words to describe what they are experiencing. It makes me think they savor their food more than I do.

Feed me a gourmet dinner and ask me how it was, I'm likely to say, "It was good," or perhaps "very good." Providing none of the foods on my plate touched, of course. I don't have words to describe what I'm tasting. It's either good and I like it, or it's not and I don't.

Though that's not entirely true; I could probably put more words to it if I tried. I've just never slowed down and thought carefully about what I tasted. I've never bothered to pay close enough attention to articulate the experience.

This is so often true of us when it comes to God's work in our lives. We read Psalm 34:8, which says, "Taste and see that the Lord is good!" (NASB). We readily agree. *Mmmm, he is surely good.* And off we go giving it no more thought.

We encounter God. We experience his hand in our lives. But we have little ability, or rather we make little effort, to describe what we are "tasting" beyond God being good. Or perhaps in those moments when we get a holy case of goose bumps, "very good."

## *What Do You Recall?*

God is working in your life. You have encountered him. He has touched you. He has spoken to you, comforted you, and led you. You know it. Yet when someone asks you about your relationship with him, what do you say?

How is your walk with God going?

"It's good."

Tell me about your year last year.

"It was good," or, "Well, there were some tough times, but God was good."

*Good* is about all we can muster. I am not suggesting that we need to become spiritual food critics, but I do believe that each of us needs to get into the habit of describing God's work in us. We need to find words to describe what we taste of his goodness.

I follow fellow pastor John Piper on Twitter. He once tweeted, "It is grievous to have a fresh insight from God, neglect to write it down, lose it forever, only to recall that it was good."

Precisely.

The moment was so meaningful at the time, we were sure we'd remember it. But as time passes, our recollection fades. And we're left with no more than a positive impression.

You've been in a church service, a Bible study, or a small group, and God was there. Or perhaps you were reading the Scriptures or listening to a worship song and God's voice seemed so clear. Maybe as you stared at God's creation in nature, you marveled at the glimpse of him. You remember the feeling and the feeling was good.

But because feeling good is often good enough, you didn't make any record of what it was that God said or did to cause the feeling. You didn't preserve it to learn from it again and again. You might remember the moment, but not the details.

I am convinced that our struggle to see God at work in our lives is not a result of his lack of work, but rather of our lack of attention to it. Our failure to take the time to articulate it when it happens.

## *Articulation*

A written record of our lives serves many purposes. It can help us to define our experiences with God. It can serve as a pointed reminder of how far he has brought us already. It can help us see our disobedience and our obedience. It is where and how we connect the dots to see our lives being transformed into his image.

The fact that we encounter God in the Word of God demonstrates the importance of articulation. God himself made the effort to write down his commands, with his own finger (Exodus 32:16).

## CLARITY

As a husband, father, friend, and pastor I feel that I am constantly communicating. Communicating love for my family, encouraging friends, leading coworkers, explaining the gospel, and casting vision. Often the busyness of everyday life sets in like a thick fog and my relationships and effectiveness suffer as a result. I want to see Jesus so clearly that the fog lifts. I want my words to be clear and to have the ability to say what needs to be said. I want to see what God sees for the people I love and lead. I am asking God for CLARITY.

*—Dean*

Journaling is not a command that we obey, but rather an example we follow in order to see God's work. The reason we have Ecclesiastes is because Solomon wrote it down. The reason we have Psalms is because David and others wrote it down. And we see Jesus in the Gospels because the disciples wrote it down. Under the inspiration of the Holy Spirit, these people wrote about the events they experienced, giving words to their feelings and beliefs.

In the Bible we see God tell his people at various times to write things down. For example, Moses was commanded to record the journey of Israel when they came out of Egypt (Exodus 32:16). And Habakkuk and John were instructed to write down the visions God gave them (Habakkuk 2:2; Revelation 1:11).

If God writes, and he tells his people to write, if he wants us to have a written record of his deeds, I, too, want to write. I want to articulate my walk with God.

### *Why I Journal*

I have learned so much about myself through keeping a journal. I've learned that my mind is prone to wander and easily distracted. I've discovered that my emotions can hijack the truth. I've seen how quickly my pride comes to the surface and how slowly my submission does.

Keeping a journal helps me see my life, guts and all. And see it in light of God's truth. I've found it the single most valuable discipline to help me see clearly. I keep at it day after day for four reasons:

1. *Writing my thoughts convinces my mind that I am serious about slowing down.* My mind races in a million directions. It needs a harness, something to rein in its restless wandering. Something to focus my sight on my heart and God's. I have found that a pen does this for me.

   I cannot write as fast as I can think, so my pen forces my mind to slow down. It's amazing what you notice, what you realize, what you remember when you take the time to. As I write, I force my mind to think about each word, each phrase, and each sentence. I do not rush it. This is as much about slowing down as it is about keeping a record.

2. *Writing my thoughts allows me to see what I am thinking so I am not blinded by what I am feeling.* Emotions can blind us. Anger, sadness, hurt, confusion, as well as the exciting feelings on the other side of the emotional spectrum, can make clear thinking difficult. I am an

emotional guy, so the pen and paper help me see what I am feeling and the thinking that's causing those feelings.

Writing through my emotions clears the way for me to think straight. Clear thinking helps me to process the truth and blow up the moments. I can identify the things I can do something about, as well as the things I can't. I can decide, rather than react.

3. *Writing my thoughts down gives me a chance to see and submit them to God's truth.* My first thoughts are not always the same as his first thoughts. Writing down what I think and what I feel serves as a confession of sorts. I just say to God, "Here I am!" Writing helps me enter the arduous process of submission. The act of submission is one that I take very seriously.

   I write my thoughts and then bring the truth of God's Word to bear on them. It goes without saying this requires that I be a student of the Scriptures. I will often write, "God, here is how I am prone to think, or here is what I would do if I were you, but I am not you, and my ways are not yours, so I surrender them." Then I pray the prayer of Christ in the garden, "Lord, not my will but yours be done."

4. *Writing my thoughts helps me to see that I am being transformed.* Surrender breaks my stubborn pride. Chronicling my encounters with God has allowed me to see myself in the light of who he is and what is true. As I read back through my journals, I can see how God has protected me from my own ways, as well as guided me in his.

   My journal is such a source of encouragement, especially during a season of difficulty. When I am frustrated with myself and want to give up, I can look back and see the story of God's faithfulness in my life written with my own hand. I can see that I am not the same person I used to be. This is such a gift!

### *What Do I Write About?*

So what do I write about?

I write what I see.

I write what I see in my heart, what I see in the world around me, and what I see in the Scriptures.

I write what I feel.

I write my thoughts and feelings and doubts and fears.

I write what I think.

I write what I think about God and my circumstances.

I write what I love.

I write what I love about my wife, my kids, my work, and my life.

I write what I believe.

I write what I believe about God, hope, and desire. I profess my belief in the promises of God. Sometimes this confession flows freely from a place of great joy, and other times I confess it to remind myself that I really do believe it.

I just write.

I record the moments I lost my temper and the moments when I wanted to but didn't. It's important to recall the great moments and the not-so-great moments.

I write about surfing with my oldest daughter, running with my youngest, or enjoying coffee with my wife. Sometimes I write about meetings or events I attended. I write about things that stress me out and things that excite me.

Sometimes my thoughts give rise to questions. I write them

down. The best way I've learned to find answers is by asking questions. A journal is a great place to write your questions. Address them to God. There is no pressure to answer them on the same page or even in the same month.

When I can't get settled and I'm having trouble remembering what it is I read in the Scriptures, I write out the verse I just read. Instead of giving up and concluding that God has nothing to say that day, I grab my pen and I write. I notice so much in the verses when I write them.

Occasionally as I am writing, the thought pushes its way into my head: *How will this make me look if other people read this?* I remind myself other people are not my audience, God is. I try not to think about how this will sound if someone reads it later, nor do I worry about whether or not what I'm writing is status-update-worthy or tweet-worthy.

In his paraphrase of the Bible, *The Message*, Eugene Peterson writes Psalm 73:1 – 3 like this: "No doubt about it! God is good — good to good people, good to the good-hearted. But I nearly missed it, missed seeing his goodness. I was looking the other way, looking up to the people."

My journal is a tool for my spiritual formation and not a place to try to impress others.

Don't try to be profound on the pages of your journal; just be yourself. This is about you, your heart, your guts, your relationship with God. All you have to do is start writing.

You are taking your thoughts seriously enough to record and clarify them. You're not writing a bestselling memoir. I don't think of myself as a writer but as someone who is willing to take the time to articulate how I have tasted and seen that God is good. This is an act of worship.

## *Diaries Are for Girls*

When I mentioned journaling at the start of this chapter, did you immediately imagine a fourth-grade girl writing in her pink-ribboned diary? Complete with a lock and a heart-shaped key?

Men in particular struggle with the concept of journaling, because we think, *Diaries are for girls!* Relax, that's why I call it a journal.

Listen, men, get a journal in camouflage or in black with spikes, but whatever you do, don't ignore this exercise. Don't miss the opportunity to see God's work in your life unfold right before your eyes in your very own handwriting.

Sports teams watch films to assess their performance and prepare for their opponents. They take notes and make adjustments in order to improve. Business people write out annual performance reviews. They make profit-and-loss statements. They want to see the facts and growth in black and white.

Whether making career decisions, financial decisions, or family decisions, whether sorting out relational issues, emotional issues, or spiritual issues, writing things down is a great way to force clarity.

As I put words on the paper, I don't just summarize events, but I work to describe them. As I write, I am asking God to speak to me and to reveal himself to me, to help me to identify his work in everything. I ask him to search my heart so I can surrender to his conviction and formation. I want to see his *work* in my life, not just see my life.

As I record my thoughts, insights, and observations, often I will see through the words on the page. The words are my words, coming from my own hand, but in them are the voice of God whispering to me, encouraging me, convicting me, and guiding me to be the person that I am created to be. I want you to experience that too.

## *Journaling Your One Word*

Use your one word to help you identify what God is doing. Write about your experience with your one word; use it as a lens to examine your days. Challenge yourself to write a couple sentences daily or weekly on your experience or progress with your word.

In 2008, my one word was KNOWLEDGE. One of the ways I planned to pursue my word was reading books on topics that were out of my comfort zone to stretch my thinking. I read everything that year from Saint Augustine's giant tome *The City of God* to Richard Dawkins's *The God Delusion*.

I created a written ledger to help me track my reading progress. It had just enough space under each day's date to record one thing I learned in my reading that day. I wrote the name of the book and a sentence or two of what I got. Sometimes I'd also record how I felt about what I read.

There were times when the accumulation of knowledge felt slow-going. I didn't feel I was learning enough or quickly enough. Frustration was rising. So I wrote about this frustration in my journal, trying to determine its source.

What I found was a sense of fear. I felt inadequate because I believed I didn't know enough. This was insecurity. I realized then that my one word KNOWLEDGE would have to be about my heart and not just about my mind.

My point is that in writing about my one word that year, I didn't just chronicle my studies. I chronicled my heart too. It brought a deeper awareness of who I am and who I'm intended to become. Through my journal, God dealt with my insecurity.

Your journal will not only be a storehouse of your experiences, but a place where you, too, will see God's hands forming your heart.

## *God's Work over the Years*

How did God form your heart last year? What about the year before that? What significant thing did you learn the year before that?

Odds are you cannot say, at least not without giving it a whole lot of thought. (Or without looking through the pages of your journal!) But I'm sure you would conclude that God was good.

By the time you are reading this book, I will have completed six years of this My One Word exercise. One of the results that I've come to regard as valuable is that I can quickly recall my list of one words. And thanks to journaling, I can describe what I have "tasted" in each of those years.

Here is a sketch of what I am talking about:

*FINISH (2007): God was building a solid sense of integrity and dependability in me.*

*KNOWLEDGE (2008): God was rooting out my insecurities and challenging me to establish patterns of being a lifelong learner.*

*AFFECT (2009): God was teaching me about the precious gift of having influence over others and was preparing my heart to deal with the challenges of my job as a pastor.*

*REGARD (2010): God was reminding me of the value of people to him and was helping me learn to value others as much as myself.*

*LIGHT (2011): This was a defining year for deeper authenticity in my marriage (my wife and I shared the same one word), and God gave me a clearer understanding of his call on my life.*

This list provides but a glimpse of God's work in my life; I could talk for half an hour on what I learned through each word and year. I see how each word has built upon the previous one. And I can recall all this because I had a single word as my focus and because I journaled my journey with each one.

What is even more incredible is that the words I chose years ago have as much impact on my life today as they did when they were my one word. *That* is heart-level change. And I know all of this because I continue to take the time to journal about it.

I have kept journals for years — since my college days. I can read them and see God's handiwork in me and my life. But I have never been able to see this broad view of God's work over the course of years as clearly and concisely as I can since beginning My One Word.

---

### HUMILITY

---

I have picked a word for five years now. This year I chose HUMILITY with the purpose of stripping away my conception of myself and recognizing how I truly appear to God. Self-deception, even unintended, keeps one separate from God. Maybe self-deception is a sin? Now after five years, I am living with five words. I am slowly corralling all my errors, misdeeds, and wrong thoughts so my deviation from a walk with God becomes less and less. And in the moment of greatest stress or temptation, I am less likely to fall completely away from God. My One Word is such a powerful life tool. I cannot imagine living without my words.

— *Scott*

## *Your Aim*

God's work in me is forged through the practice of slowing down and writing it down. This is not unique to me. I firmly believe it is true for you as well. As I have studied the lives of spiritual giants I admire, the one thing they all have in common is the fact that they keep or kept a journal.

My aim is for you is to begin this journey with a single word and a blank journal. Use those pages to record your journey, track your progress, and discern God's work in your life through your one word. Articulate the work he is doing in your own words.

Find the guts of who you are. And of who you are becoming.

There are no rules when it comes to keeping a journal. Choose one with blank pages, lined pages, or grid pages. Choose a week-at-a-glance calendar as your journal. Use a simple spiral notebook. Choose a fancy leather-bound book. Use an iPad or tablet — whatever pleases you. Maybe find one with your one word on the cover.

Just get one and write in it regularly. Remember this isn't about perfection but progress. Remember that change is possible, but focus is required. Journaling will help you focus.

I cannot say this strongly enough. No discipline has proven more helpful in seeing God's work in my life than keeping a journal. Start one and see what I am talking about! You don't have to do it, but you will likely regret it if you don't.

Learning to describe God's goodness and articulate his work in our lives is a lifelong process. But you cannot start until you start. Start getting words down on paper now, your own words.

And when I ask you how your walk with God and your one word has been, you'll be able to tell me more than "it was good."

### *Reflect*

- Get a journal and begin writing your guts out.
- Date the page and write about the past twenty-four hours.
- Resist the urge to be poetic or profound. Resist the worry that someone else will read it; use code language if you need to.

- Record your encounters with God and his Word.
- Record your journey with your one word.
- Use the exercises in this book to reflect on and explore your one word as you journal.

## Chapter 11

# WAIT FOR IT

*I say to myself, "The* Lord *is my portion;*
*therefore I will wait for him."*
— Lamentations 3:24

The waiting is the hardest part. Tom Petty sang this and I agree. Waiting on God. Waiting to discern his plans. Waiting for him to form our hearts and transform our desires.

The pace of our lives confirms our dislike for delay. So does our mood; we grow angry waiting for the car in front of us to pull out or the computer to boot up. Our impatience is also revealed in our prayers.

It seems whenever someone requests prayer we default to saying, "God, be with them." *Be with Angie as she travels. Be with Carey during the surgery. Be with Justin during the game.* And when we are heading out the door, *God, be with me today.*

There is nothing inherently wrong with this, although God has already promised he will always be with us (Matthew 28:20). But if we aren't careful, this becomes our prayer of impatience.

We become so consumed with getting where we believe God wants us to be that we forget to be with God. Our prayers amount to, *God, be with me while I do what needs to be done.* And off we impatiently run.

I am challenging you to spend an entire year with your one word. Patiently.

Why one whole year? Truthfully, there is nothing magical about twelve months. Or eleven if you spend several weeks choosing your word each year as I do.

There's nothing particular about day number 365. There is also nothing magical about January; you can begin in any month you like or in any month you find yourself.

I prescribe a period of a year with our one word for two reasons. First, we already mark our lives out in year-long increments. From calendars to anniversaries to birthdays. So a year is memorable and trackable.

Second, and most importantly, it generally takes time for our hearts to fully surrender to the change God desires to do in us. We tend to get impatient with his timing, which often leads to running ahead or forcing our way.

God calls us to be still, realizing that he is God and he is in control (Psalm 46:10). He calls us to wait on him, which often, in light of what he wants us to do, feels like a waste of time.

So if we are not patient, we can find ourselves running ahead, using this prayer to get God to rubber-stamp our own plans rather than waiting for him to bring about his plans.

I know this firsthand.

## *I've Got a Plan*

"So, Mike, what do you think God wants you to do with your life?"

The question caught me completely off guard and the truth spilled out. Like a self-inflicted bullet to my foot.

When I was seventeen, I took a job at Chick-fil-A for two

reasons. They were closed on Sunday, which meant I could go to church — a noble reason to be sure — and my girlfriend worked there. Perhaps not as noble but very compelling. (This turned out to be a good move; I married that girl five years later.)

For six years I served chicken sandwiches while attending architecture school. Through my bosses' connections, I landed an interview for a position in the architecture department at the corporate headquarters of Chick-fil-A.

I can hardly emphasize enough how badly I wanted this job. I imagined a life of scouting locations and designing future restaurants. I'd get to work with a terrific Christian-based company, putting my newly learned talents to use, and I'd have good income, benefits, and weekends off. Ideal.

Plus, if I landed this job, it would put to rest the tension I'd sensed since my sophomore year of college when I began to think God was telling me to work in youth ministry. I certainly wanted to serve kids. I loved my days as an intern in the student ministry at the church I'd grown up in. I loved the idea of hanging out and helping these young men and women through the chaos of adolescence. I just wanted to do it on my own terms.

I knew I was to serve God with my life, but I did not want to work at a church. I didn't want to deal with church politics and policies. "I just want to do ministry," was my justification. I wanted to serve my church without having to depend on them for my livelihood. Chick-fil-A was my solution.

The day of the interview arrived. I completed my sixteen-page application, wrote the required essays, and filled out the necessary forms. Now it was on to a round of introductions and meetings.

Over lunch — of chicken sandwiches, of course — I talked with two of the architects on their staff. I learned what they do and how I might fit into their organization. The more they talked, the more excited I grew. In fact, I became convinced this was God's will for me.

How much more obvious can you get? I was a Christian; Chick-fil-A is a Christian-based company. They needed an architect, and I was about to graduate as one. I could answer any question about the company's vision and values. I knew what I could offer Chick-fil-A and why I was Chick-fil-A material. I knew why I wanted to work there and nowhere else. In fact, I couldn't wait for my interviewer to sit back and ask, "So tell me, Mike, why do you want to work for Chick-fil-A?"

But that question never came.

After a round of personality testing, I sat in the office of Cleve Kiser, Chick-fil-A's director of human resources. This was finally it. The corporate big time. This was what I went to school for. I was more ready for this chance than anything I'd ever set out to do.

After a few minutes of chitchat, we got down to the interview. I am not sure if it was the first question asked, but it is the only question I remember.

Cleve Kiser looked across the desk and said, "So, Mike, what do you think God wants you to do with your life?"

*What?! You're supposed to ask me why I want to work at Chick-fil-A! What does God have to do with this? This is a Christian-based company, and I am a Christian — isn't that enough?*

I sat up straighter. As I began to answer the question, I could not believe the words that came out of my mouth.

"Well, Mr. Kiser, that is a great question. I believe that God is calling me into the ministry."

*Did I just say that? How did those words get there?*

"Well then, what are you doing here?"

"Running from God."

The truth just kept flowing.

*What in the world is going on with me? I know better than this. I prepared for this interview and I'm blowing it. I want this job!*

I looked up from the floor and made eye contact. Then I said out loud, "I don't think this is going very well."

Rather than dismissing me at that point, Kiser began to talk with me, helping me process what I had just admitted. He looked over my personality profile and told me I was well-suited for ministry work.

*Maybe so, but I am well-trained for architecture work. I don't want to start over. I don't want to have to go to seminary. I don't want to work in a church. I want this career and I want it now. God, be with me in this interview!*

I think Kiser knew I was forcing this and that pursuing this opportunity was masking my disobedience. I am forever grateful for his patience and for a company that was more concerned about me as a person than how I could perform for them.

He took my confession seriously and challenged me to stop running from or ahead of God. He encouraged me just to be with him instead.

"Do you know the last thing Jesus told his disciples to do before he ascended into heaven?"

I didn't. I searched my brain to see if I could pull out any reasonably intelligent or relatively accurate answer. Nothing surfaced. Great. First I blew the interview by confessing I felt called to the ministry. And now I was blowing my ministry cred by bombing a Bible question.

Before I could acknowledge my ignorance, Kiser offered the answer: "In Acts 1:4, Jesus told his disciples to wait."

*To wait? This is Mr. Kiser's nice Christian way of telling me I'm definitely not getting this job. Am I supposed to go sit in an upper room somewhere, cross my legs, touch my thumbs to my index fingers, and hum until Jesus appears and gives me further directions on becoming a youth pastor?*

As though he read my mind, Kiser said, "Waiting is active. Go back to what you are already doing, and do it to the best of your ability. But while you are doing it, don't focus on where you think God wants you to be, just focus on him. It is not about his direction, but his presence. Wait for him to lead. You just follow."

His words exposed my hurry. My grand plans sank like chicken nuggets in a fryer.

I had a decision to make in that moment. Would I fight for this job? Argue that I'd just gotten my degree, that I would make a good architect, and that I loved the craft? Would I insist that the best place for me to wait on God was sitting behind a Chick-fil-A drafting table?

Or would I shake Kiser's hand, thank him for his time, exit the office, and heed his advice?

Would I choose to wait on God?

---

## HELD

I chose the word HELD as my one word because that is exactly what I need to be this year. As a college student in a major that is challenging and overwhelming me, I tend to lose sight of God's hold on my life. I run around trying to accomplish all I have to do and then wonder if God is working in my life at all. *Where is he leading me? I can't see ahead. Why does he cause hardship in our lives?* The only conclusion I have come to is that through these circumstances, he is taking us and molding us into the people we were meant to be. He wants to build us into a temple where he can dwell. This year, I want to trust in his hold on my life. I want to commit my plans to the Lord and see all that he can do. I want to completely hold on to his hand as he leads me through this life. I want to be HELD.

—*Kate*

## *Another Lesson from Another Architect*

Another architect had to wrestle with this question. WAIT was Mark Loudermilk's one word in 2009. He chose it because he felt it would help him overcome his tendency to react and run when faced with difficult situations.

Mark's usual method of operation was to bail rather than deal with conflict or face hardship. He'd change companies, change neighborhoods, or change churches instead of waiting on God to guide him through the difficulty. When a crisis arose, "I'd forced my own impatient solutions," Mark explained.

So he chose WAIT and meditated on Lamentations 3:24, which says, "I say to myself, 'The Lord is my portion; therefore I will wait for him.'"

"That verse is the exact opposite of my typical human response," Mark confessed.

Fourteen days after choosing the word WAIT, Mark walked into the conference room at the architecture firm where he worked and discovered he was being laid off. Two days later, his wife lost her job as well. Mark's world seemed to crumble out from beneath him, and here he was with the word WAIT and his declaration from Lamentations.

"Even though I had no idea what was in store for me and my family, I waited on God," Mark says. "And God showed me that I could trust him."

Clients started finding Mark and hiring him. When one design job completed, another one would arise. And in the middle of a recession with the building market nearly busted, Mark started his own design company.

"Normally I would have fretted, scrambled for another job, forced my solution for the situation," Mark said. "I never would've planned to start my own company. But because I picked the word

WAIT, I had peace in the midst of my world being turned upside down."

Mark's one word afforded him rest during desperate times. Had he forced his preferred solutions in his preferred timetable, he would have missed seeing the satisfying provision of the Lord.

Lamentations 3:24 declares, "The LORD is my portion." This is the reason we wait. Our contentment is not with where we are, but who we are with. *He is enough for me* is the call of this verse and the heart of Mark's one word WAIT.

God promises to lead us and he promises to provide. But he leads us to himself and he provides his presence. We must learn to trust that he truly is our portion.

We learn this only when we abandon our attempts to have the best of both worlds. Only when we stop asking him to join us on our mission and we walk with him instead.

## *Seek Presence over Direction*

In the book of Exodus we find the people of Israel, delivered from four hundred years of slavery in Egypt, on their way now to the Promised Land. God is leading them through Moses, and he's promised that he will guide and dwell with them.

He lays out a series of instructions for governing his people and commands them to follow. Moses relays these laws to the crowd, to which they readily respond, "Everything the LORD has said we will do." (Exodus 24:3).

Moses returns to the mountaintop with God for further instruction. Only this time over a month passes.

The Israelites didn't expect him to be gone so long. They grew tired of waiting as Moses "delayed to come down" (Exodus 32:1 ESV). That is the description in the Bible.

We don't like delays. They mess with our timetable. When

things don't work out as quickly as we would like, we wonder what is wrong. We lose focus. Suspicions surface and assumptions abound. Delay often breeds distrust.

What about you? Has there been a delay in your life? A question of God's timing? Had you assumed things would be different by now? Are there places you know God wants you to go? And are you impatiently trying to force your way there?

The people of Israel were tired of waiting. Apparently forty days was their limit. They would not wait forty-one before assuming control. God's promises, presence, and plans seemed past due, so they figured it was time to take matters into their own hands.

They surrounded Aaron, who'd been left in charge, and demanded he do something. Aaron concocted a plan. He told the people to give him their jewelry and gold, and he threw it into the fire to melt it before molding it into a statue. Out pops a golden cow; this is how Aaron would later explain it to Moses (Exodus 32:24).

They built an idol in the shape of a cow. We don't build golden cows, do we? Surely we are more sophisticated than to depend on a statue.

In all honesty, my idol wasn't a gold statue, but it was a cow of sorts. A cow that held a sign that said, "EAT MOR CHIKIN!" Chick-fil-A was my golden calf. It was what I wanted to pursue, follow, and depend on, instead of God's plans for me.

Like these Israelites, we long for God to operate on our schedule. We work to figure out what God wants and to figure out how we can make it happen fast. We want to surrender our lives to God without surrendering our plans.

Do you believe God's presence is more important than his direction? It is. And this is a critical principle. One that is easy to forget or bypass in our efforts to do what we believe he wants.

When God delays, we will tend to distrust. We will lose focus. We fill in the suspicious gaps with what we would do if we were God.

My One Word is designed to help you see God's hand at work in your life over a period of time. Spending a year with your word is a way of arranging your life to resist the tendency to rush ahead with your own plans. Your word will serve as a reminder to you to wait when you are tempted to either force it or forget it.

## *Waiting for Surrender*

A season of waiting can be both painful and freeing. What I like most about it is that it's intimate. You are vulnerable before God, desperately dependent upon him.

We find we can exhale as God invites us into his presence to breathe deeply of his goodness and his grace. We don't find this sense of freedom in a hurry. That's why we spend a year with our one word. We also cannot create this sense of freedom ourselves, no matter how many of our own problems we solve or plans we achieve.

In Exodus 32, following the golden-calf disaster, Moses leaves his meeting with God and comes down the mountain to find a festival in full swing in honor of the metal cow. His anger burns. He smashes the stone tablets God had given and rails at the people for their impatient distrust.

Then Moses heads back up the mountain to meet with God and find out how he'll respond to their great sin. In Exodus 33, we peek in on that conversation between God and Moses. They are speaking "face to face, as one speaks to a friend" (Exodus 33:11 NLT).

God is delivering the bad news to Moses. "Go up to this land that flows with milk and honey. But I will not travel among you, for you are a stubborn and rebellious people. If I did, I would surely destroy you along the way" (Exodus 33:3 NLT).

When the people hear this distressing news, they begin to

mourn. Why? They are still going to get the primo land. And God is not going to destroy them. But God would not be going with them either. Suddenly they realize his presence is more important than the destination.

Moses goes back up the mountain to plead their case:

> One day Moses said to the LORD, "You have been telling me, 'Take these people up to the Promised Land.' But you haven't told me whom you will send with me. You have told me, 'I know you by name, and I look favorably on you.' If it is true that you look favorably on me, let me know your ways so I may understand you more fully and continue to enjoy your favor. And remember that this nation is your very own people."
>
> The LORD replied, "I will personally go with you, Moses, and I will give you rest — everything will be fine for you."
>
> Then Moses said, "If you don't personally go with us, don't make us leave this place."
>
> — Exodus 33:12 – 15 NLT

This encounter challenges me to rethink the way I pray. Instead of begging for direction or claiming his blessings on my plans, I am challenged to come before God and wait.

The point of Moses's prayer is clear: he would rather remain in the desert with God than head to the Promised Land without him.

As I learned to pray like this, I learned to wait on God. Waiting is not a test of patience as much as it is a test of my will.

### *How Long Do I Wait?*

Cleve Kiser was right. Waiting is an active practice. So is surrender. Waiting allows me to get my eyes off of where I want to go or where I believe God wants me to go and fix them on him. Waiting prepares me for his lead. Surrender prepares me to follow.

So how long should you wait on God? Four days? Forty days? Four years? Forty years? This is a good question.

We can't use waiting on God as an excuse for laziness or selfish inactivity. We can't refuse to follow and claim we're just waiting. We must obey when we hear his voice.

But please understand, God is more interested in your relationship with him than your usefulness to him. He has created you for himself, not just to execute his plans.

It takes time for this to sink in. Time in his presence is the only way to truly abandon your own plans and learn to trust him. It takes time for our prayers to shift from, "God, be with me as I go," to, "God, I just want to be with you where you are."

It was nearly a year from the interview in Cleve Kiser's office until God led me to become a youth pastor at a church in North Carolina. In that year I truly let go of my dreams to be an architect. I replaced my prayer of impatience with a prayer of surrender.

In his book *Shattered Dreams*, Larry Crabb explains that God often allows good dreams to shatter in order for great dreams to emerge. He writes, "Our fondest dreams for this life, the ones we naturally believe are essential for our happiness, must be fully abandoned if we are to know God."[13]

I not only abandoned my golden dream; I abandoned my schemes to keep one foot in his ways and the other in mine.

## *Waiting on His Lead Again*

A few years later, in January of 1995 according to my journal, I began to sense God prompting me to start a new church. My journal reflects my impatience to do so as soon as I sensed it.

---

13 Larry Crabb, *Shattered Dreams: God's Unexpected Path to Joy* (Colorado Springs: WaterBrook Press, 2001), 52.

"God, how long will you leave me here? I know you have called me to start a church ... let me go do it and be with me as I do."

Everything in me wanted to take off in the direction I knew God wanted me to go. The only problem was he wasn't moving yet. He wasn't going with me. I sensed his plans but I forgot to focus on his presence.

## GENTLE

My one word this past year was GENTLE. It's been an awesome journey as God revealed to me more of his character and more of his being through the revelation of my one word. What a wonderful experiment this has been! Especially to look back and realize that this word and *the* Word have become flesh in me in this process.

—*Pamela*

A year later, after agonizing over what to do and how to proceed from where I was, I wrote the following prayer in my journal. It was my Moses Prayer.

"Lord, I don't know what to do next. So you start the church, and I will do whatever you ask me to do. I'll take any role you lead me to, so long as you are there."

I'd grown tired of being where I was. I was youth pastoring at a church that was struggling. I knew God had called me to start a church; *why* couldn't I start it and get out of there?

While at a conference with my brother-in-law, I shared my frustration with him about where I was and how great it would be to finally start the church we'd been dreaming about. Chris said to me, "God won't release you from where you are until you find contentment in him there."

This became a centering statement for me. It reminded me

that my only motive to leave where I was, was to go where God was leading.

Two years later, God moved, Chris and I followed, and Port City Community Church began.

## *The Hardest Part*

I'm not surprised that PATIENCE is the second most-often picked word in the My One Word movement. It often feels in short supply. We each have to check ourselves to be sure we don't impatiently move ahead of God, regardless of our chosen word.

For our word to become a part of our character, we have to spend a prolonged period of time with it. Focus on it; pray through it; live with it. That's what it takes.

This typically doesn't happen in twenty-one days. Not in six weeks or even six months. Walk through every season of the coming year with God and your one word and see how it slowly drives deep, permanently embedding in your heart.

Your One Word will flash as a warning to keep you from forcing your will on God's. It will remind you not to run ahead — his timing is not yours. Don't use his delay as a reason for distrust. And don't lose focus in the wait — it's often the hardest part.

## *Reflect*

- Idols can be anything that we trust in place of trusting God. You read the account of my golden cow. What are the golden cows you tend to trust in? And what exactly are you trusting them for?
- We often race ahead of God when we get impatient. Or when we sense that we know where he wants us to be and we think we know how to get there. But our impatience derails us. Then we resort to praying, "God, be

with me," while missing his presence entirely. In what areas of your life do you find yourself impatient and rushing ahead, refusing to wait? A relationship? A career opportunity? A move? A major purchase? Do a gut check and root out the motive for your hurry.

- Determine what you can do to slow down, focus on God, and wait for his lead. Decide that you will remain patient and content while actively waiting.

## Chapter 12

# LAST WORDS

*For momentary, light affliction is producing for us*
*an eternal weight of glory far beyond all comparison,*
*while we look not at the things which are seen, but at the things*
*which are not seen; for the things which are seen are temporal,*
*but the things which are not seen are eternal.*

— 2 Corinthians 4:17 – 18 NASB

"Mike, cancer has blessings. Each day, I am *so* in every moment. MOMENT, that's my one word, you know."

My friend Christina told me this as we talked about her life with the disease that threatened to take over her body and identity. She wasn't putting on a brave face; she meant it. She saw each day as a gift.

Life is short. Even when we live a long, full life. Perhaps especially then. But none of us are guaranteed a long life. What we are given is the possibility of a full, abundant life.

Her diagnosis came as a cruel interruption to life-as-planned, forcing her to take it the way it comes anyway, one day at a time. Time passes — yours and mine — and when it runs out, we experience the reality of what's eternal.

Dallas Willard challenges us, saying, "We need not and must not wait until we die to live in the land of milk and honey; and if we will only move to that land now, the passage in physical death will be but one more day in the endless life we have long since begun."[14]

## REMEMBRANCE

Recently in my town a senior in high school killed himself. A lot of people went to his funeral, but there were many people who didn't know if he had been a Christian or not. I chose REMEMBRANCE as my one word because I want to be remembered as a great leader, as a good example for my siblings, as a forgiving person, as a selfless friend, and most importantly as a child of God. When people come to my funeral, that is what I want them to remember me as.

—*Sarah*

### *The Power of One Word*

It was late New Year's Eve. It's rarely a good thing when your phone rings this time of night. I answered to hear a familiar voice say, "Mike, the news is devastating."

Greg was calling from the hospital. Greg is not only a member of our church; he and his family are personal friends. He said he hated to bother me late on a holiday.

I listened in disbelief as he recounted the past seven days. His wife, Christina, had been admitted to the hospital with abdominal pain on Christmas Eve but was then released. More pain brought her back to the hospital where the preliminary scans showed some "shadows" on her liver.

The prognosis did not look good — likely to be cancer.

14 Willard, *Renovation of the Heart*, 43.

Christina was thirty-seven, the same age as my wife and me. She and Greg had four beautiful children. Their future seemed so sure, so secure. And now this. The brevity of life is felt much more sharply when it hits close to home.

I hung up the phone, told Julie the news, and headed to the hospital to step into this journey with my friend.

When you step into moments that bring death near, normal greetings fall flat. You can't simply inquire, "Hey, what's going on?" or "How's your day been?" I knew the answer to the first question and had definite assumptions about the answer to the second. As a pastor, I've walked into these situations more often than I'd prefer. But as a friend, this was my first time.

Greg stood on the opposite side of the room. I scanned his face for clues, seeking an assessment of the situation without having to ask. His expression was calm, but he was clearly processing the magnitude of the matters at hand.

Then I turned my gaze to the hospital bed holding Christina. Her face lit up with her smile. I felt immediately at ease. I said hello, leaned forward, and hugged her neck. She seemed almost excited for what she was about to tell me.

As I sat down beside her, she leaned toward me and announced, "I've already picked my one word for next year. My one word is MOMENT!"

The My One Word movement we'd begun at the church the year before was the farthest thing from my mind as I'd walked into her hospital room on that cold night with one year rotating into the next. So it caught me by surprise. I expected her to express fear or disappointment or some other emotion that typically surfaces in the uncertainty of waiting for test results to confirm if one has a life-threatening illness. Instead, her mind was on her one word, and it was clearly providing her hope.

I still stand amazed by the significance of this simple exercise, and the power for one word to become a lens through which we process whatever circumstances we face.

I watched Christina battle liver cancer over the next three years. And I saw firsthand how time and again her one word served as a handle for her to hold onto. It gave her comfort, it grew her faith, it became her prayer, and it afforded her direction, framing the vision for how she would live life now, in the moment.

## *Chasing Mirages*

Everything can change in a moment. We know this; we've heard the stories. You probably have one yourself: An accident. A diagnosis. A marriage. A loss. A lapse in judgment. A pink slip. A birth. A divorce. A test result. Our lives pivot around dramatic changes.

We prefer to operate with the myth that our lives are stable, predictable, and manageable, or at least that they will be at some future point.

As we journey through the desert of life, we chase the mirage of the oasis, living for those imaginary points in time in which everything will be good, life will finally settle down, and we will feel refreshed. And then, in the stability of that place and time, we will be able to enjoy the moment. And enjoy God.

And focus on things like spiritual growth.

It's as if we're forever on a journey to some promised land where we will finally fully dwell with God. I bet that is how the Hebrew people felt while wandering in the desert.

Moses led the Hebrew people out of slavery in Egypt. Their God-vowed destination was the Promised Land — an actual place flowing with milk and honey — where they would dwell not as slaves but as God's chosen ones.

But before they could get there, they had to learn to follow

God and live by faith according to his commands. They needed to focus on him rather than their destination. They spent some time learning this in the desert between Egypt and the Promised Land. It took forty years for them to learn to follow God. It feels like it's taken me forty years to learn as well.

I suspect that most of that time, the people passed their days dreaming of the Promised Land and feeling like their desert wanderings were a total waste.

## *Destination Thinking*

God's people are promised a land flowing with milk and honey, but on the way there they will spend time roughing it in the desert. This is true of us as well. There will be moments of angst and times of struggle that lie between the more desired places.

These are the times when we typically resolve to "just get through" and wait for it to be over. But this is, in fact, where formation happens.

It is easy to overlook these critical moments in the process. We're so busy assuming that if we can just get to where we want to be, things will get better and we will be different. I refer to this as destination thinking.

Destination thinking is our belief that our lives will be full, manageable, or happy once we get to where we think we need to be.

When I graduate from college.

When I get married.

When I have kids.

When my kids are out of the house.

When I get a new job, bigger house, different spouse.

While we're focused on this future point, our lives roll by day after day. We long to savor the moments, enjoy our lives, and connect our hearts to eternal matters, but we feel we can't, because we can't quite get a handle on the here and now. We are not yet where we need to be, and there is much to do to get there.

We try to live our lives from destination to destination, but the condition of our heart is measured in the moments in between. Your one word can help you pay attention to the condition of your heart and the moments that form it.

## *Numbering Our Days*

"Teach us to number our days," Moses prayed, "that we may present to You a heart of wisdom" (Psalm 90:12 NASB). What does Moses mean?

Does numbering our days simply mean to count them? To take a Sharpie and put a big "X" on the calendar as each day is completed? I have done this.

I numbered the days before I turned sixteen. I couldn't wait to get my driver's license, which, of course, in my mind equaled freedom. That year I numbered my 1986 calendar from 287 days down to zero.

I also counted down the days until I graduated from high school, and then college. I numbered the days of my remaining "singlehood" leading up to my wedding. Numbering our days becomes a measure of how much longer we must put up with where we are. Our eyes stay solely on the desired destination. And we miss the fact that the days in between are part of the journey, part of the process.

Have you ever numbered your days as a way to see how much longer you will live between where you are and where you wish to be?

## *Counting or Discounting?*

The words of Psalm 90 — "Teach us to number our days" — were penned by Moses. It's a prayer request from the man who led

God's people out of slavery and into the desert where he died before entering the Promised Land. These words were penned by someone who understands the danger of neglecting God's process when trying to reach the desired destination.

When I first read the prayer request, I took seriously the call to ask God to teach me to number my days, to make them count regarding the formation of my heart. My prayer became, *Lord, teach me to see each day as a critical part of your plan to change me into the man I am created to be.*

He did. In 2007, my one word was FINISH. Looking through the lens of this word, I noticed that my days often just faded out with the setting of the sun. There was no clear finish line. I wanted to finish each day well.

What would it look like to finish my days well? I was pretty sure it didn't include mindless channel hopping to see what was on before falling asleep in front of the TV with no real thought about my heart.

### PURPOSE

I want to focus on the purpose for the time that I've been given here. I want to avoid time- and energy-wasting activities that won't have any lasting impact in eternity. I want to live on PURPOSE this year.

*—April*

At the end of each day I decided I would make a conscious effort to note the condition of my heart before God and metaphorically sign my name to it. As the day closed, I imagined crossing a finish line and looking back over the distance I'd covered that day, testing my heart by my motives and actions that day. And I'd pray.

Just a quick prayer and reflection: *Lord, I want to sign my name and declare that today my heart reflected yours. Did it?* I'd let his Spirit show me the answer.

There were days when I thought, *Yes, today my heart was true. Today, I sensed your presence and heard your voice and I followed.* It felt good. My heart would fill with gratitude for God's faithfulness. And I'd praise him for his goodness.

But there were other days when I knew my heart wasn't true. As I crossed the finish line in prayer, the strongest emotion I felt those days was guilt. My first response to this overwhelming sense of regret was to write the day off, just label it "a bad day" and try to forget about it.

Isn't this what we tend to do with our failings? We want to ignore them, hoping they don't count.

Then I realized that when I wrote these days off as bad days, I was discounting the days rather than counting them. That's the exact opposite of what I was asking God to help me do.

So I started admitting this to God. As I finished the day, I would think over its events, look at the condition of my heart, and confess to him the moments when I wasn't true. And rather than spend time wishing this day never happened, I'd simply repent.

He is always faithful and ready to cleanse! His grace washed over my regret, and thankfulness rose in my heart for God's mercy toward me. It felt good. Just as on the "true days," my heart would fill with gratitude for God's faithfulness. And I'd praise him for his goodness.

These days counted. For even in these moments, my heart was being formed.

Whether it was a good day or a bad day, I'd have cause to praise God. I could praise him for the day given me and for the work he was doing in me. Each one counted.

I also noticed how apt I was, the minute one bad thing happened, to write the whole day off as "bad." The day wasn't bad. That one part may have been bad, but I was discounting all the good parts with my "bad day" label.

The day, each day in fact, was a gift. Ripe with potential to draw near to the living God and prepare my heart for him. Regardless of what happened in those twenty-four hours.

### *Accounting for Our Days and Heart*

My one word FINISH led me to find a way to number my days. Your one word can also keep you aware of the heart-forming process and remind you that each day has purpose. No matter your age or condition, each day does have great purpose. Richard Bach wrote, "Here is a test to find whether your mission on earth is finished: if you are alive, it isn't."[15]

Every day is a key part of God's plans for you. Each one is a gift, an opportunity to further develop a heart of wisdom.

So "number" each day. Not to count them up or down but to take into account the formation of your heart in the moments that tick by. The moments both good and bad. Ask God to give you this perspective and to teach you how to number your days—value them, live them—so that you can present your heart to him.

### *Beyond Our Numbered Days*

The normal, natural pace of our lives will not likely lead us toward spiritual formation. This principle is one of the foundations My One Word is built upon. We aren't going to drift toward spiritual formation, toward developing a heart of wisdom. It has to be chosen and done.

---

15 Richard Bach, *Illusions: The Adventures of a Reluctant Messiah* (New York: Random House Digital Ink, 1989), 59.

My One Word offers a tool through which you can choose it and do it.

Our chosen words provide lenses through which we can see God's work in our lives over the course of a year. They're lenses that help us see what is happening in our hearts. But they can also help us keep eternity in view.

One more observation from this psalm by Moses. "Teach us to number our days" is the request. You can only count things that are countable. Taking an inventory implies a limited supply of that which is counted. This includes our days on earth.

We number the finite, for the sake of the infinite.

"Life is not about finding our limitations; it's about finding our infinity," legendary jazz musician Herbie Hancock supposedly once said. Finding our infinity—why would this be something that human beings crave? The answer is found in Ecclesiastes 3:11: "He has made everything beautiful in its time. He has also set eternity in the human heart."

Every human heart longs for the eternal.

Nonetheless, we have a short-sighted habit of trading the infinite for the finite. We forget that we are living in a temporary time and space, headed for an eternal home. We rush through moments seeking to get to the next earthly place or the next accomplishment, where we expect to finally be satisfied.

The constant pressure caused by our destination thinking and our sense of hurry has a way of hardening our hearts and blinding us to eternal matters. However, if we learn to see with an eternal perspective, we will notice that every moment has potential. Even the struggles and disappointments are preparing our hearts for a joy we cannot imagine.

Paul writes in 2 Corinthians 4:17–18: "For momentary, light affliction is producing for us an eternal weight of glory far beyond all comparison, while we look not at the things which are seen, but at the things which are not seen; for the things which are seen are temporal, but the things which are not seen are eternal" (NASB).

Human eyes naturally focus on what attracts or distracts. The pleasures of this world leave us chasing after the next thing. And the struggles stir in us a desperate desire to escape to someplace else. Someplace next. Either way, we fall into destination thinking. We fix our eyes on what's next, forgetting our eternal Promised Land, and forgetting that this moment is all we truly know we have here.

---

**AWAKE**

---

I feel like I have been living my life in a fog. Not really awake to each day, not really awake to opportunities, challenges, and most of all blessings. I will not—*I will not*—sleep through the rest of my life.

*—Barbara*

### *Her Last Word*

In January, three full years after the discovery of the shadows on her liver, Christina's condition took a grave turn for the worse. Despite her tenacious fight, the cancer was exacting its toll.

After weeks of finding it difficult to function, she was heading back to the hospital for more experimental treatments. I had the honor of traveling several hours with her and Greg to a top-notch hospital in our state. It was the first I'd seen her in the new year.

When they picked me up at my office, I hugged them both and jumped in the car. Before we even got out of the parking lot, Christina brought up My One Word.

"My word this year is FINISH," she declared.

I swallowed hard.

She explained how she was viewing her life in ever smaller increments and cherishing the completion of each one. "I don't want to leave anything undone. I want to finish," she added.

Although she told me she was not talking about dying, I believe she was preparing to finish the race she'd been given to run. Christina had that awareness.

The treatments relieved some of the pain but did not stop the cancer. In April Greg and Christina received the final prognosis from the doctors.

Just over two weeks later, I sat down with Christina to talk about the finish line. Our conversation was calm and tender, yet intense. As she spoke, I watched her eyes; they were so clear. I can still remember the clarity of her eyes. She told me what she wanted to say to those who would soon gather to mourn her death and celebrate her life.

She wanted me to tell her friends, neighbors, and family to test their faith, to determine what they hold onto and what truly sustains them. She wanted them to examine the condition of their hearts and decide if they were relying on the next earthly destination to provide their hope, or if they were anchoring their hope in Christ.

She wanted to say to them, "Whatever happens to you along the way to where you are seeking to be, when things don't work out the way you want, and when the days that you are supposed to be numbering seem without hope, '*will you withdraw and become bitter about it, or will you draw near to God and bring him glory?*'"

Those were her exact words. Her words were not about status or accomplishments or whether or not you had arrived where you wish you were. Instead, she spoke of the condition of the heart.

Christina loved My One Word. She was such an ardent fan of

this exercise. The four words she chose during the course of her battle reveal the process by which she learned to hold fast to her faith and trust God with her life. Indeed they showed her heart of wisdom.

She chose MOMENT the year she was diagnosed. That year she learned to be mindful and thankful for every part of each day. The next year her one word was INSPIRE. Her courage and grace in the face of her struggle were certainly an inspiration to many.

As her battle seemed unbearably long, she next chose the word IMPOSSIBLE. Only she wrote it like this: I'M-POSSIBLE. It was possible for her to live in the face of death. And should death take her body, it could not destroy the eternal life that lay endlessly before her.

In 2011, her word was FINISH. It was her last word.

Five days after my conversation with Christina, she passed away at the age of forty-one. She was a wife, a mother of four, a friend to many, and an inspiration to all.

I knew I would have to stand before her friends and family and bring a sense of closure and comfort, but most of all, I would have to bring hope. When things like this happen, people desperately need hope. In moments of loss and grief, everyone's heart longs to believe in something beyond what we can see.

Giving them this hope was a task Christina would take upon herself to complete.

---

## MOMENT

Every day, if we pay attention, God has a MOMENT for us ... changing a diaper, telling someone about Jesus. Not every moment is equal, but God teaches and shows us his will every day. And in that we have our MOMENT!

—*Paul*

## *Rooster Friends*

I told the following story at Christina's funeral because it reminds us that our lives are made for the here and now, but even more for the ever after. The eternal is more real than we can know.

Elizabeth was one of Christina's dear friends. They called themselves "rooster friends." That's what Elizabeth told me the day after Christina died. We were talking because I couldn't believe the story I'd heard, and I called to ask her about it.

They referred to themselves as "rooster friends," because they both lived life with a little swagger. Roosters are prone to strut and make noise to let you know they are alive. This inside joke stuck, and the rooster became the mascot for Christina and Elizabeth's friendship.

They'd exchange cards with drawings of roosters on them. They'd give each other trinkets with the barnyard bird as tokens of their friendship. Elizabeth had given Christina a rooster ring. Christina had worn it daily as a constant reminder of her friend. As Christina's body withered from the disease, the ring wouldn't stay on her finger. So Elizabeth wore it for her.

As the disease progressed and Christina's strength waned, these two friends began to discuss what would happen when Christina's days here on earth were finished. The conversations got serious.

They spoke of Christina's husband and her four children. A mother's love is a powerful thing. She'd fought hard during her last three years. She fought for her children; she fought for her husband; she fought for the life she'd been called to live. She fought with a heart full of faith in Christ.

As Christina and Elizabeth talked, Elizabeth made a request. She wanted to know, once Christina passed on, that Christina was in heaven and was no longer suffering or worrying and that heaven was truly the most beautiful place she'd ever seen. Christina had impeccable taste, and Elizabeth knew that if Christina said it was beautiful, then it surely was. They decided that Christina should send her a sign.

"Just send me a picture of a rooster somehow to let me know you are there and that it's wonderful. Like, put the picture on the side of a poultry truck that passes me on the road. When I see the rooster picture, I'll know you are in heaven, and your heart is at peace in the most beautiful place you've ever seen."

"I'll do better than that," Christina responded. "I'll send you a real, live rooster."

They laughed and cried, soaking up the closing moments of a treasured friendship.

On May 3, 2011, Elizabeth was chaperoning a field trip to a farm out of town with her elementary school class. As they toured the pig pens, the cow pastures, and the horse stalls, a rooster began to follow Elizabeth around. Everywhere. The other adults and kids noticed.

"Ms. Elizabeth, that rooster really likes you!"

She took out her phone and snapped a picture to send to Christina. This would be funny.

She sent the text with the photo at 10:17 a.m.

No response.

Later that day Elizabeth got a call from Greg. He told her that her "rooster friend" had passed away that morning.

"What time?" Elizabeth asked.

"About 10:05."

### *Finish Well*

I shared this story with the crowd at Christina's funeral, and I share it with you to awaken in us all a needed sense of the eternal. That is the Promised Land.

I told those gathered that day that God sent a rainbow following the flood to remind us of his promise. That he sent a dove following Jesus' baptism to remind us of his presence. And perhaps, at Christina's request on May 3, he sent a rooster to remind us of the hope of eternity with him.

I can almost hear Christina saying, "I told Elizabeth I would let her know. I had to FINISH what I started. I didn't leave any loose ends. FINISH, that's my one word, you know!"

Our lives here are short. The Bible reminds us of that. And one event, one diagnosis, one decision can forever alter our normal way of life. But so can one word.

Don't wait until you know you have only a few days left before you begin counting your days. Use My One Word. Choose your word now, keep your word now, number your days now, and make them count by developing a heart of wisdom this year.

Finish well, friends. Finish well.

# VIDEO DISCUSSION GUIDE

Welcome to the discussion guide for *My One Word: Change Your Life with Just One Word*. We're pleased that you're engaging with the accompanying video for the My One Word project—good move.

The My One Word video study is designed to be used in a group setting such as a Bible study, Sunday school class, or any small group gathering.

It's not necessary for each person in the group to answer every question, but everyone should participate in the weeks' discussions and share their one word with the group. So prepare to be vocal, even if you're typically the quiet type. (Week four of the video series touches on why your group is vital in your My One Word project.)

Each group should appoint a facilitator who is responsible for starting the video and keeping track of time during discussions.

Facilitators, please remember that the goal is not to just get through the questions, but rather to engage in the process of God's work in the life of each group member. Use the discussion questions to guide the conversations and to better understand how God is forming the people in your group. This is a *guide* for discussion, but your aim is to follow the Holy Spirit's directive as you lead the group.

A recommended reading schedule is provided. Following the recommended reading schedule will allow your group to complete the book in the course of one month. However, the discussion questions are based mainly on the messages presented on the videos so you can read the book at your own pace if needed.

Are you ready to change your life with just one word? Let's get started!

### *Week One: The Power of Personal Vision*

The project you are embarking on is one of choosing just one word to be your single focus for an entire year. Talk briefly as a group about any reservations you may have about setting aside your list of ways you want to change in favor of focusing intently on just one word — just one thing — for an entire year.

#### VIDEO

Play the video segment for session one. As you watch, you may want to take notes on anything that stands out to you.

#### GROUP DISCUSSION

1. Mike described feeling so busy doing life that he didn't have time to live it. And more importantly, he didn't have time to focus on the spiritual condition of his heart. Can you relate to feeling overwhelmed with stuff to do, learn, manage and improve?

   What is currently cluttering your "I-should-do" list?

2. Spiritual formation rarely happens in a hurry. As Mike explained, the normal, natural pace of our lives will not push us toward spiritual formation.

   Amidst the appointments, the home maintenance tasks, your family responsibilities, the tyranny of technology, and your daily work, how well — on a scale of 1 to

10—are you monitoring your heart and engaging with Christ in its renewal?

a. What is helping you in that quest?
b. What prevents you from engaging in the process of formation? (Discipline? Time?)

3. According to the BARNA research group, over 90 million Americans currently make New Year's resolutions. Given that large number, it's safe to assume we all have things we'd like to change.
    a. Have you made New Year's resolutions in the past? What were they? As a group, make a list of all the New Year's resolutions you can remember making.
    b. Did you succeed with any of them? Discuss why you failed or succeeded.

4. What characteristics come to mind when you think about someone with "personal vision"?
    a. Do you feel you have a strong personal vision for your life? Or specifically for the coming year?
    b. How much does your personal vision drive your daily decisions? Discuss what tends to drive you.

5. This week you will start the process of choosing a word to focus on for the coming year. Consider starting a My One Word notebook or journal. Use it as a place to think through the directions in the Pick Your Word chapter; use it to take notes during the video sessions; use it as a place to answer the questions at each chapter's end throughout the book; and use it to chronicle your year with your one word.

Do you journal? What are your thoughts on or previous experiences with journaling?

## CLOSING

Close together in prayer. Be sure to pray for God's guidance upon all group members as they each seek to choose their one word for the year ahead.

## BETWEEN SESSIONS

Read the introduction and chapters 1–4 of *My One Word.*

If needed, re-read chapter 3 this week as you narrow down your list to choose your one word.

## *Week Two: It's a Process*

## CHECKING IN

Before watching this week's video, go around the room and share your chosen one word with the group. Tell a little of why you chose it or what your hopes are for this year with this word. Also tell at least one way you plan to keep your word in front of you this year.

## VIDEO

Play the video for session 2. As you watch, you may want to take notes on anything that stands out to you.

## GROUP DISCUSSION

1. Think of a time when you decided to quit trying because you were frustrated or felt you were not getting where you should be quick enough. What was that situation and what became of it?

2. This year-long one-word journey is about the process of transformation — and process always takes time.

   Pastor John Ortberg says, "Waiting is not just something we have to do until we get what we want. Waiting is part of the process of becoming what God wants us to be."[16]

   Identify a time in your life that you successfully completed a lengthy process in order to reach your goal. What was it, and how did the process shape you?

3. Have someone read Hebrews 12:1 – 3 aloud.
   a. In verse 1, what does the writer instruct us to do to prepare for the race we will run this year?
   b. In light of your one word, what are your roadblocks or hindrances?

4. Have someone read 1 Corinthians 9:24 – 27 aloud.
   a. How does your one word help you set a clear goal(s) for this year?
   b. What discipline will be required for you to continue in the direction of your vision?

5. What stood out most to you from either your book reading this week or from the video message?

6. Mike talked about his troubled friend who worked in the trucking business and had unrealistic expectations about how long it would take to change at the heart level. Mike's friend also failed to recognize that relatively small changes (like "just be nice") can actually produce enormous results over a long period of time.

16 John Ortberg, *If You Want to Walk On Water, You've Got to Get Out of the Boat* (Grand Rapids: Zondervan, 2008), 179.

Share one small action with regard to your one word that you will begin making this week. (If you're in need of some ideas, let the group suggest some.)

## CLOSING

Close in prayer. Pray for perseverance in this year-long process of spiritual formation.

## BETWEEN SESSIONS

Read chapters 5 – 8 of *My One Word.*

Place your one word in several places where you'll see it this week. Post it to your bathroom mirror, set it as your home screen on your phone, put a sticky note on the dashboard of your car. Then follow through with the one small action you committed to making this week.

### *Week Three: Resistance Builds Strength*

## CHECKING IN

Take a few minutes to discuss how it's going with your one word — share any stories, victories, struggles, or insights so far. Also report on the outcome of the "one small action" you committed to begin last week.

## VIDEO

Play the video for session 3. As you watch, you may want to take notes on anything that stands out to you.

## GROUP DISCUSSION

1. In this session, Mike explained that resistance builds strength — both in the gym and in life. Yet we tend to long for the path of least resistance.

On a scale of 1 to 10 (10 being embracing it and 1 being throwing the covers over your head) how well do you handle struggle?

2. What tempts you to veer away from your one word project?

3. Mike told a story about how he learned on the volleyball court that when someone expects to struggle, he or she can prepare in advance for how to handle it. Consider and discuss how you can prepare yourself for the temptations that you know you'll likely face regarding your one word.

4. What does your one word require from you when you encounter resistance?

5. Have someone read Hebrews 12:1–4 aloud.
    a. What are we to fix our eyes on as we stay in it for the long haul with our one word? Why fix our eyes there (according to verse 2)?
    b. What does verse 3 reveal can give us the strength to avoid becoming weary and quitting?
    c. Verse 4 in the ESV reads: "In your struggle against sin you have not yet resisted to the point of shedding your blood." How does that put your present difficulties or struggles to embody your word in perspective?

6. There will be times this year that each of us "fails" at remembering our one word or at embodying the vision it represents. Failure, however, does not have to paralyze you. As a group come up with a working definition for "failure" that will keep you from feeling paralyzed by it.

## CLOSING

Close in prayer. Pray for the ability to endure the inevitable struggles that lie ahead while keeping anchored to your one word.

## BETWEEN SESSIONS

Read chapters 9 – 12 of *My One Word.*

### *Week Four: Your Community & Your One Word*

## CHECKING IN

Congratulations! If you followed the recommended reading schedule, you've completed the *My One Word* book! Take a few minutes to discuss what stood out most to you in this book.

## VIDEO

Play the video for session 4. As you watch, you may want to take notes on anything that stands out to you.

## GROUP DISCUSSION

1. Mike said that often he'd prefer to "row alone." He confessed that, like most of us, it's easier for him to just show up, look nice, be nice, and wish everybody a nice day before going home and closing the garage door. Discuss how this common modern tendency contrasts with the way Jesus lived.

2. Have someone read the following verses aloud.

   - Romans 12:15
   - Galatians 6:2
   - Philippians 1:2 – 5

   Can we rejoice and weep with others, help them bear life's unexpected hardships, or care about others as much as ourselves by looking nice, being polite, wishing everybody a nice day then going home and closing the garage door?

Tell about a difficult time when someone stepped into your life and helped you hang on by holding you or helping you for longer than you admitted you needed them to. What impact did that have on you?

3. According to Mike, what is "crowded loneliness"? Tell of a time you have felt this yourself.

4. Mike told the story of a crewmate who, upon realizing his oar had broken, jumped out of the boat to spare the group his "dead weight." Mike explained that that may be fine in a sports competition but not in the Christian life. Be gut-honest with yourself and the group on this question. Do you allow others to see you struggle?

   In what ways do you pull back from community when you feel broken?

5. Accountability requires honesty. And being accountable to one another requires taking each other seriously.
   a. Are you prone to make people play detective when it comes to your struggles or fears?
   b. Who do you proactively share your struggles with? Who in your life has permission to ask you about your struggles?
   c. Will you give this group permission to at least call you out of isolation when you retreat?
   d. What are some specific things your friends could ask you in order to help hold you accountable to keeping your one word?

6. Outside of your group, who have you told about your chosen one word? Have you shared this idea with any nonbelievers?

   Tell some people this week about your word and this My One Word project.

**CLOSING**

Determine how your group will continue to discuss your one words this year so the accountability factor of this project remains high. Mark the calendar to do periodic My One Word check-ins and make them a regular part of your meetings.

Personally consider how you will use others' one words to spur them on. And spur them on!

Close in prayer. Pray for each member of the group with specific regard to their one word.